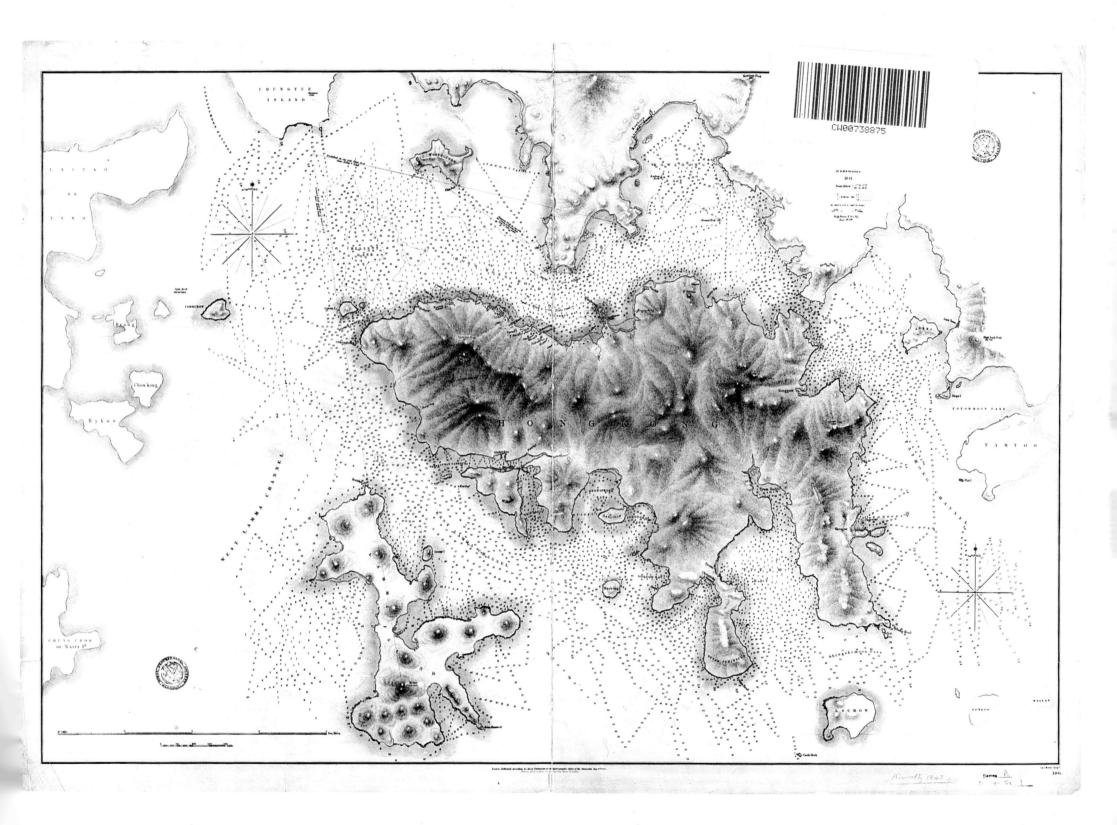

WHITE ENSIGN ~ RED DRAGON

THE HISTORY OF THE ROYAL NAVY IN HONG KONG 1841-1997

2nd edition

Edited by
Commodore PJ Melson CBE Royal Navy

WHITE ENSIGN ~ RED DRAGON

EDITOR: *Commodore PJ Melson CBE Royal Navy*

EDITORIAL COMMITTEE:
Kevin Broadley, Kathleen Harland, James McGowan
Janet Melson, David Tait, Ruth Vernon

PUBLISHER: *David Tait*
ASSOCIATE PUBLISHER: *Lieutenant Commander K Broadley Royal Navy*
PRODUCTION DIRECTOR: *Calum Gordon*
RESEARCH EDITOR: *David Dunbar MBE*
COPY EDITOR: *Colin Ogg*
PROOF READERS: *Francine Martin, Larissa Downes*
BOOK DESIGN: *Calum Gordon*
PRE-PRESS CONSULTANCY: *Kerry Nelson, Ryan So, Jack Kok*
MARKETING: *Jacqueline Ratnavira, Jilly Davies, Joanne Braithwaite*
COVER DESIGN: *Gillian Peacock*
PRINTED BY: *Prontaprint Asia Ltd, Hong Kong*

All rights reserved © 1997
Royal Navy
Edinburgh Financial Publishing (Asia) Limited

ISBN 962-7982-24-5

Compiled and published for the LEP Trust by

Edinburgh Financial Publishing (Asia) Limited
Suite 1007, 10/F Wing On House, 71 Des Voeux Road Central, Hong Kong
Tel: (852) 2869 8969 *Fax:* (852) 2804 6492

THE LEP TRUST

Hong Kong Chinese personnel have served with the British Forces since the mid-19th century, in peace and in war. The Royal Navy has had a large complement of Chinese sailors amongst its ships' companies while the Army has been served by the Hong Kong Military Service Corps. Together these sailors and soldiers are known as Locally Enlisted Personnel (LEP).

On 30th June 1997 the British Garrison will leave Hong Kong; the majority of the LEP will remain behind, having been made redundant. It was decided that a Trust Fund should be established to provide assistance to any of these ex-servicemen and their dependants who find themselves in hardship, distress or poverty.

The Trust, which was launched on 5th December 1993, is run by a board of military and civilian trustees. We are now in the process of raising funds to make it viable; indeed all the proceeds from the sale of this book will be given to the Trust. The target is to raise a minimum of HK$35 million by 30th June 1997.

CONTENTS

I am delighted to contribute to this important book, which describes the vital role played by the Royal Navy in the founding and the history of Hong Kong. In 1841 Commodore Bremer first raised the Union Flag on the barren rock which became Hong Kong. The first governor was Captain Charles Elliot R.N. There followed a continuous Royal Naval presence in Victoria Harbour until the Japanese occupation of the Colony during the Second World War. The ending of that occupation was due in no small part to the brave efforts of the task force under the command of Admiral Harcourt who, after the liberation, became the second Naval governor of Hong Kong. From 1945 to 1997, the Royal Navy has kept continuous watch in the waters of Hong Kong, playing a crucial role in combatting smuggling, piracy and illegal immigration. It is a stirring story, familiar to those who served on the old China Station, but now disappearing in the mists of time. This book preserves that story for history.

The Royal Navy in Hong Kong has always enjoyed a particularly close relationship with the local community and Locally Enlisted Personnel have served alongside their British counterparts, on shore and sea, throughout the century including both World Wars and the Korean War. It is a fitting recognition of their contribution that profits from the sales of "White Ensign, Red Dragon" will go to the Locally Enlisted Personnel Trust, for the benefit of those ex-Royal Naval Chinese sailors remaining in Hong Kong after 30th June 1997.

香港總督府　　　GOVERNMENT HOUSE
HONG KONG

On 22 June 1793 HMS Lion, carrying Lord Macartney, Britain's first emissary to China, passed just to the South of Hong Kong Island. Speculation as to what would have happened if Macartney had succeeded in his mission - to establish equitable trading relations with China - constitutes one of the most interesting 'what if's' in relations between East and West, but it would have left us the poorer for the Royal Navy's distinguished association with Hong Kong. The Navy led the British merchants cast out from Macau and Canton to the settlement of Hong Kong. They provided the earliest detailed maps of the place - the hydrographic work of Captain Belcher in 1841 was of such high quality that much is still in use today - and they provided the security under which trade by merchants of all nations could take root in Hong Kong.

This book takes the story of the Royal Navy in Hong Kong from those early days through the great changes of each passing year. Hong Kong today stands as a monument to what has been made possible by freedom of the seas, a cause that the Royal Navy has extended and sustained so well. It will remain so even as the Royal Navy closes its base here and departs with the change of sovereignty at midnight on 30 June 1997, and the memory of all that the Royal Navy has given to Hong Kong will remain too.

Governor

v

INTRODUCTION

This book is the culmination of an idea which germinated in the minds of some of the last Royal Naval officers to serve in Hong Kong. We were aware that much of the unique history of our service in the Far East lay in the museums and libraries of the territory, which would be difficult for us to access after 1997. In addition, we felt strongly that we needed to raise money for a trust fund for our Locally Enlisted Chinese Sailors, most of whom were retiring without a pension. The result is *White Ensign ~ Red Dragon*, the proceeds from the sale of which will be donated entirely to the LEP Trust.

I cannot pretend that this is a definitive history of the Royal Navy in Hong Kong. The subject matter is vast and there is a huge amount of source material available to research. However, much as a detailed history is needed for reference, it is unlikely that such a book would have allowed us to raise the sum we require for charity. Since we intend to raise money through book sales, we have selected this format as being both the most attractive and the most likely to appeal to a wide and interested readership.

I invite you to read about the founding of the Colony after years of dubious trade in opium, and how the Royal Navy has interacted with the people of Hong Kong and the South China Sea throughout a turbulent century. From Odious Opium, through Communist Conundrums, to the End of an Era, this book, with its marvellous photographic record, traces Hong Kong's transformation from a 'barren rock' to the powerhouse of commercial success that it is today. Some of the extraordinary photographs from naval archives – notably those of the Japanese surrender in Hong Kong – have never been published before.

To those who have contributed material, literally from the four corners of the globe, I would like to say thank you. Everyone involved in the production of *White Ensign ~ Red Dragon* has done so in their own free time and, in these dying days of the British Empire, there is far less of that than any of us would like. As the deadline for publication approached the material continued to flood in and we had far more than we could reasonably use. We have been able to pick and choose from this wealth of information and I hope we have succeeded in producing a book that is both balanced and readable. Above all, I hope we have done justice to the generations of our naval predecessors who did so much to make this last great Colony what it is today, and that the Locally Enlisted Personnel and their families will continue to benefit from the LEP Trust.

ACKNOWLEDGEMENTS

Much of *White Ensign ~ Red Dragon* is based on a previous publication, *The Royal Navy in Hong Kong 1841-1980*, written by Kathleen Harland in 1982. She has generously allowed us to use some of her original text, research and photographs. Without her, the production of the book would have been immeasurably more difficult, if not impossible.

I owe a huge debt of thanks to David Tait, an ex-Royal Navy submarine officer and the Managing Director of Edinburgh Financial Publishing (Asia) Ltd, who put a great deal of his own time and energy into the book's production. His publishing team selflessly gave their own time and professional publishing knowledge to the project. Of the many individuals involved in the production team, Calum Gordon, the Production Director, deserves particular recognition, as does David Dunbar MBE for his research and for ensuring that the Royal Marines were far from forgotten. The book was printed at cost price for which I am more than grateful to Clive Howard, the Managing Director of Prontaprint Asia Ltd.

My editorial team of Lieutenant Commander Kevin Broadley, my wife Janet, Ruth Vernon and Jim McGowan have all worked exceptionally hard, and I pay tribute, in particular, to Kevin Broadley for the vast amount of work he has put into the project. In addition, three Royal Naval Reserve officers serving in the UK spent much time researching and writing for me in Hong Kong: Lindy Mackenzie-Philps, Penelope Utting and Chris Seaton progressed the compilation of material considerably during their respective attachments.

I am also very grateful to Richard Hownam-Meek for the considerable effort he has made in producing an impressive, almost definitive, chronology of Royal Navy ships that have served in Hong Kong on the Far East Station.

Our sponsors have been many and various, and are listed separately following this, but I would particularly like to thank Sir Donald Gosling of National Car Parks and the Royal Hong Kong Yacht Club for their exceptionally generous donations. Jardine Matheson and Swire Pacific graciously recognised their long association with the Royal Navy in Hong Kong through very considerable contributions to the LEP Trust, as did both the Furama Hotel and the Conrad International Hotel, Hong Kong.

P J Melson CBE
Commodore Royal Navy

SPONSORS

Without the generosity of the following sponsors, the publication of *White Ensign ~ Red Dragon* would not have been possible:

The Gosling Foundation
The Royal Hong Kong Yacht Club
Furama Hotel Enterprises Limited
The Conrad International, Hong Kong
Edinburgh Financial Publishing (Asia) Limited
Prontaprint Asia Limited
John Swire and Sons
Jardine Pacific Limited
Jardine Matheson Limited
ABN AMRO Hoare Govett Asia Limited
Serco Gardner Guardian Merchant
Lloyd's Register of Shipping
BZW Asia Limited
Modern Terminals Limited
HKR International Limited
Black Isle Communications (Hong Kong) Limited
Harilela Foundation Limited
Lachmibai Gopaldas Trust
Mr JM Gray CBE

CONTRIBUTORS

Commodore Melson and his Editorial Committee are indebted to the following organisations and individuals for submitting text, photographs and anecdotes used in the book:

Lieutenant Commander Charles Addis RN	Mr RSS Hownam-Meek
Mr Colin Aitchison	Illustrated London News Picture Library
Lieutenant Commander Simon Ancona	Joint Service Public Relations Staff,
Leading Photographer L Baverstock	Hong Kong
The China Fleet Country Club	Captain Peter King, Trinity House
Mr Mike Critchley, *Maritime Books*	Lieutenant Commander G May RN
Director of Public Relations (Navy)	Commander R Palistre RN
Lieutenant N Doyle RN	Lieutenant Commander Mel Petrie RN
Leading Airman Photographer C Fford	The Public Records Office, Hong Kong
Mr Tom Henderson	Mr Tim Reeder
Flag Officer Surface Flotilla	Lieutenant T Redfern RN
The Fleet Air Arm Museum, Yeovilton	Professor Sam Richardson
FormAsia Books Limited	The Royal Naval Museum, Portsmouth
Sergeant K G Gray	The Royal Hong Kong Yacht Club
Lieutenant D Grey RN	John Swire and Sons
Mr J Hanratty	Mr JM Wattis, Wattis Fine Arts
Lieutenant Commander R Hanslip RN	Mr David Watts
Rear Admiral JR Hill	Mr Richard Webb, Richard Webb Limited
Colonel RM McGarel-Groves RM	Captain David Whitehead RN
The Hong Kong Museum of Art	The United Kingdom Hydrographic Office
The Hong Kong Museum of History	Hilary Cree
Senior Superintendent T Hollingsbee,	LA (Phot) Craig Leaske
Royal Hong Kong Police	

By far the biggest contributor to the book is Kathleen Harland who is an author in her own right and has written several books, including a history of the Queen Alexandria Royal Naval Nursing Service and an historical novel based around the Norman Conquest. She is currently working on a doctoral thesis at Exeter University on the development of Royal Naval Hospitals from 1700. She lives in Budleigh Salterton, Devon, with her husband, a Royal Naval Surgeon Commodore whose sojourn in Hong Kong first encouraged her to write the original history, *The Royal Navy in Hong Kong 1841-1980,* published in 1984.

ODIOUS OPIUM

A SMALL ISLAND IN THE SOUTH CHINA SEA

The presence of the Royal Navy in Hong Kong has been inextricably linked to the protection, development and prosperity of this small island in the South China Sea. British governance has enabled the 1,074 square kilometres that comprise Hong Kong Island, Kowloon and the New Territories to evolve from a sparsely populated area of southern China to a thriving city of six million people and an economic power of global status. The Royal Navy has continuously facilitated this evolution.

By the mid-18th century the city of Canton had become an established centre of trade with the West. Throughout the 18th and early 19th centuries, enterprising British merchants managed to develop an extremely lucrative, albeit illegal market, selling opium to the Chinese. By far the greatest quantity of the drug came from British-ruled India.

Conference between Sir J J G Bremer, a Chinese admiral and the chief mandarins onboard HMS Wellesley on 4th July 1840, in the harbour of Chusan. Drawn by Sir Harry Darell, lithograph by J H Lynch. On the basis of the convention agreed, the Royal Navy made its first formal landing on Hong Kong Island. [HK Museum of Art]

Successive Chinese emperors took the not unsurprising view that opium was harmful, and had banned its use and distribution for many years. The British, however, conveniently and consistently ignored these laws. In March 1839, the Special Imperial Commissioner for the Suppression of the Opium Trade, Lin Tse-hsu, arrived from Peking. Within a week Lin took hostages and demanded the surrender of all British-owned opium in Canton, a staggering 20,291 chests of it.

Harried merchants sought refuge downstream in the Portuguese colony of Macau, and when sanctuary was denied by those authorities, they took shelter among the many vessels moored off the nearby islands, of which Hong Kong was one. In September 1839, the traders wrote to the Government asking for prompt intervention and retaliatory action against the officials in Canton. Given the circumstances, this had to be in the form of Royal Navy troopships and men-of-war.

The position of Canton on the Pearl River meant that any initial retaliatory action would have to be naval bombardments. By 1840, 17 warships and 27 troopships were anchored in Hong Kong harbour. The expedition was commanded first by Rear Admiral Lord George Elliot and later by Commodore Sir Gordon Bremer, while the Admiral's cousin, Captain Charles Elliot, was given the grand title of Plenipotentiary, in essence the first Governor of Hong Kong.

Naval action began in January 1840. British troops bombarded into submission and occupied the forts controlling the narrow channel leading to Canton. This was sufficient to force the Chinese to the negotiating table, and a cessation of hostilities agreed. This treaty (although never actually signed) is known as The Conference of Chusan.

On the basis of this flimsy document Elliot authorised a naval party, under the command of Commodore Bremer, to land and formally take possession of Hong Kong Island on 26th January 1841. Elliot's decision, however, did not meet with the approval of the British Government, and he and Bremer were called home in disgrace. Nevertheless, they probably fared better than their Chinese counterpart, who was sent back to Peking in chains.

A degree of ambiguity surrounded these initial actions, and the situation was still not satisfactorily resolved. The British Government was determined to find a permanent solution, and despatched a new team from England. Admiral Sir William Parker and Sir Henry Pottinger (who became the second Governor) were tasked with establishing a suitable base from which the British could continue trading, unhampered by the Chinese. They quickly concluded that this could only be achieved by force.

A combined Navy and Army expedition took Amoy, Tinghai, Chusan and Ningpo on the Chinese mainland. In the spring of 1842 the Chinese counter-attacked at Ningpo. Not only was this manoeuvre unsuccessful, but it prompted the British fleet to bombard the Woosung forts, continue up-river to capture Chinkuang and block the Grand Canal, before laying off outside Nanking.

With the British fleet victorious, the Chinese were once again forced to the negotiating table. By the time the treaty of Nanking was signed in August 1842, British merchants had gained the freedom of trade they so desired. As the treaty itself stated:

It being obviously necessary and desirable that British subjects should have some port whereat they may careen and refit their ships when required and keep stores for that purpose, His Majesty the Emperor of China cedes to Her Majesty the Queen of Great Britain . . . the island of Hongkong, to be possessed in perpetuity by Her Britannic Majesty, Her Heirs and Successors.

(Top) The signing and sealing of the Treaty of Nanking, 1842 - Captain John Platt, engraved by John Burnet. [HK Museum of Art]

NAMES

Of the principal Officers and Official Gentlemen who are represented in the Engraving of the Signing and Sealing of the Treaty of Nanking in the State Cabin of H.M.S. Cornwallis, 29th August, 1842.— The time chosen by the Artist was after the Treaty had been signed and sealed, and while the Admiral's Band was playing the National Anthem on the Deck.

1. Major Shirreff, C.B. D.A. General.
2. The Hon. H. Keppel, R.N.
3. Lieut.-Col. Mountain, C.B. Adj.-Gen.
4. Sir Thomas Herbert, K.C.B. R.N.
5. Major-Gen. Lord Saltoun, K.C.B. G.C.H.
6. Frederick Kingsmur, R.N.
7. H.E. Lord Gough, G.C.B. Commander-in-Chief.
8. H.E. Sir H. Pottinger, Bart. G.C.B. H.M. Plenipotentiary.
9. Kwang, Sec. to the Chinese Commissioners.
10. Elipoo, Imperial High Commissioners.
11. Keying, Imperial High Commissioners.
12. K. N. Thom, Esq. Interpreter.
13. H.E. Sir W. Parker, G.C.B. Commander-in-Chief.

14. Haou Ling, the Tartar General.
15. Lieut.-Col. Malcolm, C.B. Sec. of Legation.
16. Captain P. Richards, C.B. R.N.
17. Lieut.-Col. Hawkins, C.B. Com.-General.
18. Lieut.-Col. Wilson, C.B. Paymaster of the Forces.
19. Sir R. Bartley, K.C.B.
20. The Hon. F. Grey, C.B. R.N.
21. Major Moore, C.B. Judge Adv.-General.
22. Capt. Collinson, C.B. R.N.
23. Capt. Bentley, 6th D. Adj.-General.
24. Capt. Watson, C.B. R.N.
25. Capt. Tuker, R.N.
26. Capt. Morsford, D.A. Com.-General.
27. Capt. Halsted, R.N.
28. Com. M'Cleverty, R.M.

29. Dr. Grahame, Surgeon to Commander-in-Chief.
30. Lieut.-Col. Fawcett, C.B. 55th.
31. Capt. Kingcome, R.N.
32. Capt. Cunynghame, A.D.C.
33. Lieut.-Col. Campbell, C.B. 98th.
34. Major Grant, C.B. M.B.
35. Subadar Major, M. Sappers, A.D.C.
36. Lieut.-Col. Gough, C.B. Quarter-Master-General.
37. Dr. Woosnam, Sec. to Sir H. Pottinger.
38. Capt. Gabbutt, M.B. Artillery, A.D.C.
39. Hon. John Morrison.
40. The Rev. Charles Gutzloff.
41. New Keen, L.H. Commissioner.
42. Com. Tennant, R.N.

43. B. Christon, Esq. R.N. Sec. to Adl. Parker.
44. Com. Skipwith, R.N.
45. G. T. Lay, Esq. Interpreter.
46. Capt. Frederick, R.N.
47. Capt. Bethel, R.N.
48. Capt. Ball, R.N.
49. Lieut.-Col. Blundell, C.B. Madras Artillery.
50. Lieut.-Col. Pratt, C.B. Cameronians.
51. Major Pears, C.B. Madras Engineers.
52. Com. Maitland, R.N.
53. Lieut.-Col. Lloyd, C.B. Bengal Volunteers.
54. Major Anstruther, C.B. Madras Artillery.
55. Col. Montgomery, K.C.B. 18th.
56. Lieut.-Col. Knowles, C.B. Bengal Royal Artillery.

To dinner upon may the Treaty be landed.

R. G. JONES, PRINTER, WEST HOUSE COURT, GREAT STREET, LONDON.

3

Our first footing in Hong Kong; the island pronounced British Territory, January 20, 1841.
[Illustrated London News Picture Library]

POSSESSION

The first naval officer to set foot on Hong Kong Island was probably Sir Edward Belcher, Captain of *HMS Sulphur*. He recalls the landing in his book, *Narrative of a Voyage Round the World, Performed in HMS Sulphur*:

> On the return of the Commodore [to Macau] on the 24th [January 1841] we were directed to proceed to Hongkong and commence its survey. We landed on Monday, the 25th 1841 at 15 minutes past 8 am and being the bona fide first possessors, Her Majesty's health was drank [sic] with three cheers on Possession Mount. On the 26th the squadron arrived; the marines were landed, the union [sic] hoisted on our post, and formal possession taken of the island by Commodore Sir JJG Bremer, accompanied by the other officers of the squadron, under a feu-de-joie from the marines and a royal salute from the ships of war.

The place where Bremer landed came to be known as Possession Point. At the time the sea extended to the current day Queen's Road, and so it is probable that where Possession Street meets Queen's Road Central today is the actual landing site. Although a small park on Hollywood Road, which is at the southern end of Possession Street, is probably close to the landing site, no plaque or commemorative stone was ever placed to record the event.

The line of Queen's Road was established very early in the colony's history. It followed an old track used by junk crews who had to pull their craft along the foreshore when the wind failed.

Hong Kong from Kowloon, 1843 - Thomas Allom. [Wattis Fine Arts]

HMS Plover *and* Young Hebe, *1842. [HK Museum of Art]*

Captain Belcher's name is well preserved. There is Belcher Street, Belcher's Gardens (an apartment block) and Belcher Bay. His ship, *HMS Sulphur*, from which the first survey and chart of the island was made, is also remembered through Sulphur Channel, which lies between Green Island and the western tip of Hong Kong Island.

The second landing was further east. Captain Belcher took his first readings near Morrison Hill, and named the principal surroundings accordingly. Again, the event is remembered in a street name, Observation Place, which runs from Hennessy Road to Morrison Hill Road. In 1911 the street was renamed Tin Lok Lane, which means Happy Heaven Lane. It connects with Happy Valley, which is

situated at the southern end of the street. The original reference for the surveys, a bolt from the sloop *HMS Rifleman*, is still in place in the former *HMS Tamar* (renamed the Prince of Wales Barracks in 1993), making it the first chart datum in the new colony.

SETTLING IN

As early as April 1841 the naval authorities began to erect buildings along the foreshore. The first naval store sheds were at West Point and Possession Point, and early maps reveal that major construction was also carried out at another, slightly more westward site, between 1845 and 1855. Store depots were also quickly established onshore, and the first naval Storekeeper and Agent Victualler, Thomas McKnight, was appointed on 21st March 1842. He held the post until 12th October 1849.

The Navy also made use of ships moored in the harbour. *HMS Minden*, originally a hospital ship, was used as a store ship from 1846. During the Second China War (1857-59), *HMS Princess Charlotte*, a three-deck, 100-gun ship of the line, was sent out to act as a Receiving Ship. These ships had specific

functions, one of which was to provide office and living accommodations. The Commodore certainly used it as an administrative base in the 19th century, as well as a home for his family. Official salutes on formal occasions such as the Queen's Birthday, were usually fired from the Receiving Ship. Plays and musical evenings were also held in the ship, as was the more serious business of courts martial.

The Navy, in the early days of Hong Kong, was thus very much an afloat organisation. Naval personnel lived onboard, thereby avoiding the worst ravages of the diseases that laid waste the Army ashore who, in numerical terms, lost a battalion to sickness every three years.

From Hong Kong, the ships of the China and the Far East Station were deployed to support trade on the China coast and to continue survey and administrative work deep into the Pacific. Within the protective shadow of the Royal Navy, the great Far Eastern trading hongs prospered and grew. As a result, the Royal Navy soon realised that it needed more than a Receiving Ship and a few matshed storerooms to support its Far Eastern deployments.

In the very early days all the ships on the China Station were wooden sailing ships, usually third rates

The Harbour of Hong Kong - from an original sketch, 27th December 1856. [Illustrated London News Picture Library]

HMS Princess Charlotte *in the 1830s. It was Admiralty regulation that hammocks should be aired when in port. [Kathleen Harland]*

that carried between 60 and 74 guns. An exception was the first rate *HMS Melville*. A one-time flagship of the East Indies Squadron, she ended her days as a hospital ship and was sold in 1873 to pay for the new Royal Naval Hospital.

A permanent China Squadron was established in 1844, but for many years it consisted of no more than six ships, enough to tackle pirates and enforce the trading rights finessed at the treaty of Nanking. The treaty ports of Canton, Amoy, Foochow, Ningpo and Shanghai had a brig each, and Canton, the nearest and busiest, usually had a steamer. Brigs were small, light vessels ideally suited to coastal work.

A frigate and a steamer were stationed at or near Hong Kong.

The real workhorse of the Navy in Hong Kong in the 19th century was undoubtedly the gunboat, which was rather more than a boat with a gun on it. The term was applied to various types of steamers, all well armed and suitable for river work. Not long after the Crimean War (1854-56), larger gunboats, called gun vessels, were built, although newspaper accounts frequently referred to them as gunboats. Larger ships, such as HM *Ships Audacious* and *Victor Emmanuel*, were exceptions to this classification. Among the larger vessels, a few are worthy of special mention, given their close connections with the station over a number of years.

HMS PRINCESS CHARLOTTE

Launched at Portsmouth on 14th September 1825, the *Princess Charlotte* was a first rate vessel of 2,443 tons and 104 guns. Named after the daughter of King George IV (better known as the Prince Regent) and Caroline of Brunswick, the Navy Lists show the ship stationed at Portsmouth, not yet in commission, until 1837. Although such a situation may seem strange now, it was not so at the time. In the post-Napoleonic era the dockyards continued to turn out large numbers of wooden sailing ships, but there was

simply not enough work to go round, and perhaps not enough money either, as in peacetime the government always cut back on military spending. In 1837, she was worked up to become the flagship of Admiral Sir Robert Stopford, Commander-in-Chief Mediterranean. It was then that she gained her single battle honour, at the bombardment of St Jean d'Acre on 3rd November 1840. After service in the East Indies she was sent to Hong Kong in 1858.

HMS VICTOR EMMANUEL

Laid down in the Pembroke Dock in May 1853, her original name was *Repulse*, but this was changed in 1855 while she was still on the stocks. Almost certainly, this was intended as a compliment to King Victor Emmanuel II of Sardinia who, in 1861, became first king of a united Italy. Classed as a screw ship of the second rate, she was 230 feet long and 55 feet broad, and carried 80-90 guns. *Victor Emmanuel* carried troops to Africa and the Far East before arriving in Hong Kong on 4th November 1874. There seems to have been a hand-over period of a month when both she and the *Princess Charlotte* were listed as Receiving Ships. Then, on 11th December, the *Victor Emmanuel* appears in the shipping lists as the sole Receiving Ship, in the

On the eve of the Japanese attack, orders were issued to sink any potentially useful vessels. HMS Tamar was scuttled four days after the Japanese crossed the border. At first the vessel, which had become a familiar landmark resolutely refused to sink and the Royal Artillery were called in to hasten her demise with dynamite. [HMS Tamar, FormAsia Books Ltd]

charge of Commodore JE Parish, with her armament reduced to a mere two guns. In 1878, when Governor Hennessy visited Commodore Watson, it was to this ship, and not to any establishment ashore, that he was invited to 'stay to tiffin'.

Over a period of 21 years, the ship became a well-known feature in the harbour: from her masthead flew the Commodore's broad pennant; from her decks salutes were fired in honour of arriving and departing warships; and from her offices the day-to-day business of the Navy in the Far East was conducted. Illustrations of that era show that roofing for extra space and shelter in bad weather covered her upper decks. This certainly gave her a distinctive silhouette.

HMS Victor Emmanuel, *1855. [Kathleen Harland]*

 # HMS TAMAR

The 3,650-ton ship from which Hong Kong's naval shore establishment derived its name was built at Millwall and launched at the beginning of June 1863. She set out on her maiden voyage on 12th January 1864 as a troop-ship to the Cape and China. The Royal Navy had not yet fully changed over to steam power, and consequently *Tamar* was originally barque-rigged, i.e., she had three masts: the fore and main were square, and the mizen fore and aft rigged. Later, however, *Tamar* was equipped with a steam engine that allowed her to do about twelve knots. An early photograph shows her with two funnels, but she was later re-boilered and reduced to one funnel.

The ship's crest was based on the coat of arms of the county of Cornwall, which the river Tamar divides from Devon. To have taken the whole arms would have breached copyright; consequently, the base of the crest of *HMS Tamar* has only 10 bezants (roundels) instead of the 15 found in the arms of Cornwall. The wavy lines are self explanatory.

HMS Tamar first visited Hong Kong in 1878 with relief crews for the gunboats. Before that she had seen service off the Gold Coast, taking troops to the

Ashanti War. One death and one birth occurred on the seven-week passage out from Portsmouth. Her stay was short, and she soon departed for Singapore to pick up the 74th Highlanders, who were to relieve the 28th Regiment, then stationed in the colony. *Tamar* returned only once, in 1886, before her final return in 1897, when she relieved *Victor Emmanuel* as Receiving Ship. At first, the ship was moored at a buoy in the harbour, but from 1913 she was kept alongside the west wall of the dockyard's basin, with only occasional moves for docking or to test her sea-worthiness.

Though the First World War scarcely affected Hong Kong it was very different with WWII. When it became clear that the Japanese attack could not be halted, orders were issued that any type of vessel that could be useful to the enemy was to be put out

1844 Regatta painting [The Cree Journals]

of action and sunk. *Tamar* was one of the first to go. As Commander Crowther recorded, she was taken out of the basin and sunk at a buoy on 12th December 1941.

The actual scuttling was not easy, as the superstructure built over her decks to provide administrative accommodation became airlocked. For some time a sizeable portion remained resolutely above water. Finally, the Royal Artillery was called in to finish off the job.

Hong Kong Island from the north.

Lymoon Pass and part of Kowloon.

In the great days of sail, coastal views were a major aid to navigation. These three views were drawn in 1846 by Lieutenant LG Heath of HMS Iris. They were published in 1847 with the title Views of Hong Kong Island and Vicinity *and supplemented Commander Belcher's original chart. [The Hydrographic Office]*

Outlying islands, including Stonecutters and Lantau, with a number of frigates moving around in the anchorage.

The North East View of the City of Victoria, Capital of Hongkong, *24th June 1843 - Prendergast. [Wattis Fine Arts]*

The Combined Fleet in China - Transports in Cowlong *[sic]* Bay prepapring to get under way for the north. *[Illustrated London News, 1860]*

PIRATES ON
THE CHINESE MAIN

With Hong Kong's development as a colony and major commercial centre, ensuring that trade and shipping could run free from any interference was of paramount importance. The biggest threat to the shipping industry came from the swarms of pirates operating in the China Seas. The sheer scale of these operations is astounding. In fact, the Portuguese used to call the area around Hong Kong Island the *Islas Ladrones* – the Pirate Islands.

One of the most infamous and powerful pirates prior to the arrival of the British was Cheung Po Tsai, who was based in Hong Kong between 1806 and 1810. He had a fortified lookout post on Victoria Peak, and from there directed the operations of his 270 fighting junks and 40,000 men. The Imperial Chinese administration of the period made attempts to curb Cheung's operations, but he was so powerful they could not defeat him. He eventually received a huge bribe to keep the area quiet on their behalf!

The real danger to traders of all nationalities, however, lay on the high seas beyond Hong Kong and off the China coast. Legally, the authorities were able to tackle pirates at sea, but not within Chinese coastal waters to a range of three miles. The geography of the locality, with its many bays, inlets and estuaries weighed heavily in the pirates' favour. It was also official policy that pirates could only be arrested if caught red-handed. At first, the Chinese Government rejected offers by the Royal Navy to co-operate in suppressing piracy outside Hong Kong waters. They maintained that all Chinese waters came under their jurisdiction and that such co-operation would amount to a loss of face. Politically, therefore, the British Government could only effectively concentrate on local Hong Kong waters, and chasing individual pirate vessels remained very much a hit-and-miss affair. When Captain Collinson of *HMS Plover* commandeered what he took to be a pirate junk, he was criticised for behaving aggressively.

When the first gaol opened in Hong Kong in October 1841, 10 months after the formal establishment of the colony, it was, according to records, 'filled with pirates awaiting trial'. They and others captured in the vicinity of Hong Kong in the years that followed were, relatively speaking, the lucky ones. If a pirate was captured by Chinese Government forces he would have his justice meted out in swift traditional fashion – execution by beheading.

Colonial administrators frequently asserted that the suppression of piracy should be a police, rather than a naval, responsibility. This view though was not supported by sufficient funds for the water police to expand their role to any significant extent. The first record of a separate 'marine' division of the police force is in 1845, when a Water Police unit of 14 officers was formed to patrol Victoria Harbour in a rowing boat. The Royal Navy therefore continued to shoulder much of the burden of anti-piracy work, but on an operational level there was effective co-operation between the Royal Navy and the police.

A very early example of the liaison between the two forces was the work of Daniel Caldwell. A former seaman from the lonely Atlantic island of St Helena, Caldwell arrived in Hong Kong in 1841. He was from an ethnically mixed background, was multi-lingual and could pass himself off as Indian, Chinese or European. Employed in the rank of Assistant Superintendent of Police, Caldwell became a brilliantly successful naval intelligence agent. His assiduous gathering of information on shipping movements and the location of pirate fleets resulted in many successful anti-piracy operations.

Paradoxically, as the pirates' organisation improved, the Navy's task become easier. In the

'The Eaglet and the Auckland's boats destroying Mandarin junks in Toong-Chung' *and* 'The blowing up of the Chinese Commodore's junk, and burning of others, at Toong Chung'. *[ILN 9th May 1857. Wattis Fine Arts]*

'The Eaglet's attack on Chinese junks at Toong-Chung' *and* 'Return of the Eaglet to Hong Kong, Dressed in the Chinese Flag' *[ILN 16th May 1857. Wattis Fine Arts]*

1850s and 1860s set piece battles were common, where naval skill and discipline told against sheer audacity. One such running battle took place between 28th September and 3rd October 1849 and involved *HM Ships Columbine, Fury* and *Medea* and the junks of the then-number-one pirate chief, Chui Apoo. The result was the destruction of Chui's entire fleet of 23 junks, each armed with 12 to 18 guns and manned by 180 buccaneers. Two mini-dockyards on remote islands where the pirates had repaired and replenished their vessels and men were also destroyed.

A few weeks later Commander JC Dalyrymple Hay led another successful attack. His assault force consisted of *HM Ships Phlegeton, Fury, Colombine* and a large number of officers and men from *HMS Hastings*. The objective this time was the number-two pirate chief, Shap-ng-tsai. These two actions resulted in the greater part of the pirate force being eliminated.

Local merchants showed their gratitude for the victories by donating a 'suite of plate worth £200 to each captain present at this action'. Although in those days this was a princely sum, the money represented only a small proportion of the value of cargoes saved, indicating the scale of piracy at the time.

A third pirate fleet was destroyed by *HMS Rattler* on 10th May 1853 and a fourth by *HMS Barracouta* in 1854. An eyewitness account of this expedition provides an excellent picture of what running a pirate fleet to ground entailed.

THE BATTLE OF KUHLAN

On the 11th November [1854], the Barracouta, *with two Imperial [Chinese] junks left Hongkong – [note the old spelling of Hongkong; the modern form, Hong Kong, was not authorised by the government until 1926] – to join the expedition sent against the stronghold of Kuhlan in the island of Tylo. We met HMS Spartan and got an armed boat from her, and anchored at night near our destination. Next morning at daylight we weighed anchor and soon joined the expedition, consisting of HM Ships Encounter and Styx, the US steamer* Queen, *and the Peninsula and Oriental Company steamers* Canton *and* Forbes, *with the Winchester's launch in tow, a very important force. The small steamers of light draught were necessary owing to the shallowness of the bays and the imperfect surveys of the island and soundings about Tylo.*

On passing the island of Cowcock, we descried three junks making all sail towards land, endeavouring to escape, their guilty conscience hurrying them. Faster-faster! Overboard went the guns one after another: anything to lighten them. Three boats were sent in chase from the Spartan *and* Barracouta *with the Winchester's launch. Before the boats reached them, the pirates had left the water and were now scampering up the hills, occasionally taking a rest and a last look at their junks and booty, all speedily committed to the flames.*

We found that the large steamers could not get within five miles of Kuhlan, so it was determined by Captain O'Callaghan of the Encounter *to proceed in the morning with the small steamers towing the armed boats of the expedition. Mr Sarrat of the* Spartan *spent the greater part of the night in a small boat sounding the bay of Kuhlan within musket shot of the piratical fleet. Long before daylight on the morning of the 12th I was roused from my slumbers by the rattling of muskets and cutlasses, each man procuring his own arms. Our paddleboats with a 24-pounder howitzer in each, and pinnace with a 12-pounder, were ready alongside. Having dressed and swallowed a cup of coffee I took up my position in the pinnace, with my side-arms and surgical instruments. The small steamers towed the boats within 2,000 yards of the pirate fort and cast them off. In the meantime, the Portuguese war lorcha [a vessel*

Peninsula & Oriental Steam Navigation Company Ship Canton *towing the becalmed* HMS Columbine *into action against pirate junks, 1849.*
- Norman Wilkinson [P&O]

with a European-type hull but a Chinese rig], *Amazona*, *armed with ten howitzers sailed in and anchored within six hundred yards of the fort. She had just joined us from Macau.*

The island of Tylo is about fifty miles to the south west of Hongkong and twenty south of the Portuguese settlement of Macau. It is irregular in shape and very hilly, one range of hills extending the entire length on the north, another on the south, and between them a pretty valley winds round jutting rocks, spreading occasionally into broad paddy fields, and narrowing again for the passage merely of a fresh-water stream. At either end of the valley is a sandy beach, dry for a considerable distance at low water, and at full tide a large boat could get within two hundred yards of the shore. On the west, both ranges of hills jutted out for about eight hundred yards into bold headlands and formed the boundaries of a crescented bay; on the side of this an artificial basin with locks was formed for the reception of junks requiring repair, and near it, fifty piratical junks were at anchor.

An embankment was thrown up from side to side, behind which twenty guns peeped from their embrasures; this protected the approach to the village of Kuhlan, which was built on a gentle inclination of the north side of the valley. The homes were very good and uniform in size and, for a piratical village, very neat. The pirate flag, black, waves from every eminence, and at each embrasure

The warrant appointing Acting Lieutenant Henry Alphonsus Arundell to Her Majesty's Commander-in-Chief East India and China Stations 1859-62. [Colin Aitchison]

of the fort a man stood waving the flag of defiance.

Ere the armed boats had reached within range of the fort, the pirates opened fire with all their guns on the little lorcha. The latter treated them with contempt, not deigning to return a single shot till she received the signal from Captain O'Callaghan to 'engage', when with quickness and precision, she returned the fire. The line of boats also opened fire, advancing as they fired.

In the meantime, a party of marines under Lieutenant Burton landed on the north side, accompanied by a rocket party. Finding the fort getting too hot to be comfortable, the pirates gradually slackened their fire and a large number of them issued forth to meet the marines, who were steadily advancing on the fort. The boats, running aground, were left in charge of boat-keepers, whilst the crews, with musket and cutlass, took the water, and were soon on shore.

About two hundred of the pirates retreated to a battery near a temple placed on an elevated terrace, whilst the rest scampered away in all directions, chased by Blue Jackets. Those in the battery, urged to fight by the exhortations of their chief who was arrayed in a robe of scarlet, maintained their position till fairly driven out by the bayonets of the marines.

The Portuguese and the Americans were conspicuous in the affray: the former attaching themselves to the marines who were about to scour the island. The Blue Jackets had taken possession of the junks and were preparing to set fire to them; a work for which they are pre-eminently adapted: they like to see a good blaze, it accords with their joyous dispositions. From behind rocks and shrubs gingall balls came dropping around in all directions.

The day grew hot and bright and, as the marines, with our allies, passed to the other end of the valley, the firing became desultory. I accompanied this party. We examined each house and hamlet we passed; some of the cottages were filled with fowl and pigs, scarcely a soul was to be seen, save an old man or woman to [sic] old to

run. After some heavy marching we reached a creek communicating with the sea. In it were moored twelve boats resembling whale boats, but larger, and capable of living in any sea; in such as these the pirates boarded the Caldira. [This is a reference to a recent piracy.]

A handsome temple with a few straggling cottages stood on the beach close to the creek. The cottages were filled with nets, ropes, hawsers and many articles plundered from honest traders. The interior of the temple was richly decorated with banners of fine silk, gongs, tom-toms, spears and a fine sprinkling of josses on an altar gaudily painted and gilded. Anxious to propitiate Buddha they had a fair repast for this divinity of oranges, cake and tea; and incense was burning before him. On this occasion all their gods appeared to have deserted them, vanishing in flames, which in a short space of time left but the bare walls standing.

There was a halt, to rest and refresh the inner man with whatever our haversacks produced. A portly editor, a little out of breath, with sun-burnt visage, sat apart on a bank with a large joss, his trophy suspended from his neck, busily engaged in committing to paper the events of the day; with laudable zeal he always tried to witness any little affair of a warlike nature, and even the bright rays of the sun failed to quench his literary ardour.

A most amusing incident occurred during the day. The officers, on leaving their respective vessels, provided

themselves with haversacks and whatever food the ships afforded: some were satisfied with a little biscuit and cold pork, with a flask of rum, others with something more delicate. A Mr B had provided himself with a roast fowl, cold ham, case of cheroots and a flask of brandy, but in his anxiety to land from one of the boats he took up the wrong haversack, containing a humble supply of biscuit and pork. A group of officers were collected together, lying at ease under the shade of some wild pine, when Mr T, to our infinite amusement, drew forth from Mr B's bag the fowl and concomitants. The worthy owner was far away on some other part of the island, so we drank his health in the brandy and very much relished the cheroots – and the joke.

We resumed our search and returned to the place of embarkation about four o'clock where we found the force with a fair display of prisoners, our Chinese allies taking care of the captured guns: the only duty the gallant braves performed during the day. Presently we were joined by Captain Rooney of the Caldira armed to the teeth, laden with some of his discovered property, and driving before him four pirates. We enquired how he managed to capture so many. 'Faith,' replied the warm-hearted Irishman, 'didn't I surround them?'

Captain O'Callaghan publicly thanked Lieutenant Scarnachia and the gallant crew of the Portuguese lorcha Amazona for their conduct during the day. We then embarked on our boats, having to wade out to them, and in an hour were comfortably located on board the ships, and steaming away from the much humbled stronghold of Kuhlan. It is needless to state that for a considerable period afterwards not the sound of a pirate's voice was heard on the water; those who escaped from Kuhlan joined the Chinese rebels.

One fine young American Marine, belonging to the US frigate Macedonian *lost his life, some say by accident, others from a gingall ball. We conveyed his remains to Hongkong in the* Barracouta. *On the 14th [the same day] we left Hongkong and cruised amongst the Ladrone Islands for some days, but saw no more of our piratical friends.*

And so ends this fascinating account of the first expedition against Kuhlan. That it failed to subdue the pirates completely was borne out by the need for another expedition the following year.

The Navy continued to fight piracy where and when they encountered it. The regular onslaughts became classified under the heading 'fire brigade' tactics. With the arrival of Admiral Sir James Stirling, the new Commander-in-Chief, the war against the pirates was pursued with increased vigour. He requested and received eight small shallow-draught gunboats sent out from Britain in 1856. Most of these new arrivals went into action between September 1858 and March 1859, not only capturing

upwards of 13 junks, but destroying a pirate village, battery and slipways. Admiral Stirling also began to organise convoys, whereby a number of merchant ships were escorted together to their destination under the protective guns of the service.

During the governership of Sir Hercules Robinson (1859-65) the character of piracy changed. Marauding fleets no longer roamed the coastal waters looking for stray merchants, but instead carried out carefully planned attacks on selected targets. The Governor wanted the Commander-in-Chief, Admiral Kuper, to have four gunboats constantly available for anti-piracy work. The Admiral, however, took a different view. He felt that the

Kowloon pirates in stocks …

… awaiting execution …

… after execution. [Officers' Mess POWB]

civil government should do much more to control shipping in the harbour. With no proper system of licensing, innocent-looking merchant ships could be, and were, turned into pirate vessels in one of the many quiet coves of the mainland. There was further complaint of the ease with which pirates were able to buy their arms and ammunition locally. In short, the Admiral felt that his ships were being called on for duties that an efficient colonial police force should have been performing. Kuper's concerns must have been acknowledged in Government circles, since the new Governor, Sir Richard Macdonnell (1866-72), began carrying through certain reforms: all ships had to be registered; their movements within the harbour and their anchoring were controlled by the government; and all junks entering or leaving were inspected before being given clearance.

These reforms marked a significant change in the official attitude that pirates were solely a naval problem. The reforms depended for their efficiency on a strong water-police force – exactly what the Navy had been demanding for some time. The efforts of Governor Macdonnell to combat piracy in local waters were certainly effective, and it ceased to be a chronic problem. It was not totally eradicated, however, and isolated incidents continued well into the 20th Century.

On 10th December 1890, the British coastal steamer *Namoa* became the first victim of a new, more sophisticated kind of piracy. Pirates would hi-jack vessels on which they had embarked as deck passengers (sometimes high-ranking pirates would travel luxury class), smuggle guns onboard, blend in with the rest of the passengers and when the signal was given, seize control. They would then sail their prey into pirate strongholds like the notorious Bias Bay, and offload the booty onto their own junks.

Curiously, for the next 23 years, there was no more *Namoa*-type piracy. Inevitably, fear gave way to reassurance, which was succeeded by complacency. Then a series of similar piracies occurred, harassing British and Chinese ships for the next 20 years. Although naval vessels still went on 'pirate patrol', increasingly the problem was left to the Water Police.

Until 1904 the Water Police had been administered as a minor adjunct of the Hong Kong Police. In the same year a Naval officer, Assistant Harbour Master Commander Basil Taylour, was appointed Assistant Superintendent of Police. His brief was to enhance the efficiency of the force and eliminate the duplication of responsibilities between the Harbour Master and Police departments. Taylour's tenure as head of the Water Police was short-lived, as funding to make his post permanent was not appropriated. A precedent however had been set.

On 24th May 1909, Taylour's successor as Assistant Harbour Master, Lieutenant Commander Charles Beckwith, was appointed to command the Water Police. A Manxman with a distinguished service record, he had been in the Far East since his appointment as Navigating Officer of *HMS Diadem*, on the China Coast station, in 1905.

The capable and energetic Beckwith adopted a radical approach, reorganising the Water Police along contemporary naval lines. Training and certification in navigation and engineering disciplines were formalised and regular instruction in law, communications and weapons handling was introduced. New launches armed with machine guns were commissioned, and the creation of four geographical sea divisions facilitated patrolling Hong Kong's outer waters.

Beckwith relinquished command of the Water Police when he was promoted to Harbour Master in 1920. His legacy was an organised, efficient and professional Water Police force, far better equipped than that of a decade earlier to deal with the rampant lawlessness in and around Hong Kong waters.

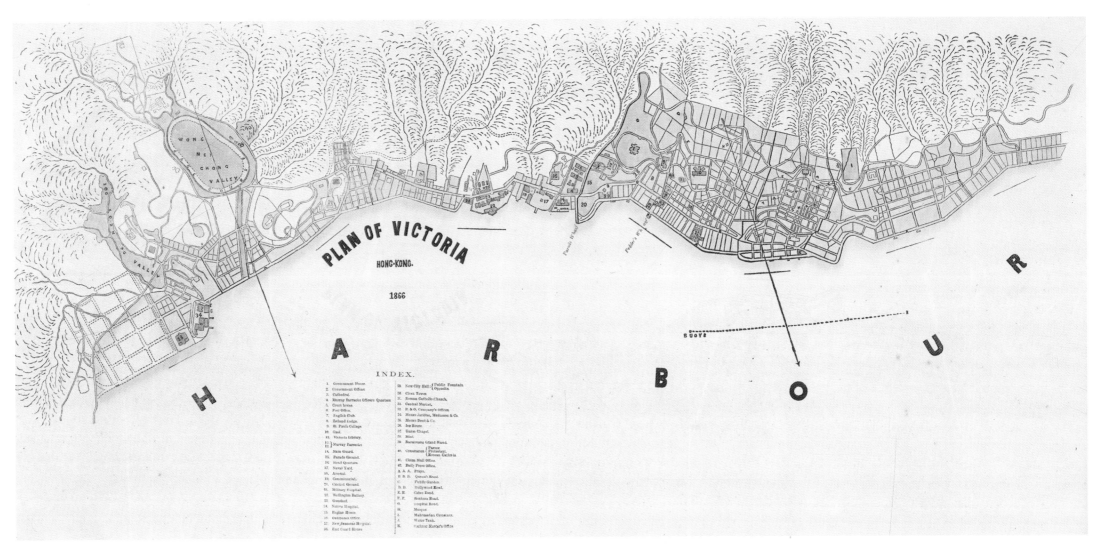

Plan of Victoria, Hong Kong, 1866, William Mayers. [Wattis Fine Arts]

During the fighting with the Japanese in December 1941 most of the Water Police fleet was sunk, captured or scuttled. Many of the captured vessels were taken away by the Japanese for use in China.

The real post-war revival of the police fleet began in 1948. Large-scale recruiting and specialist training provided the manpower for a number of ex-naval and ex-air force vessels. These craft were handed over by the departing military administration in 1946 to what was now called the Marine Police. Since then, the Marine Police and the Royal Navy have developed a lasting relationship. The detailed local knowledge, legal support and constabulatory powers of the former, linked with the operational experience of the latter, have ensured an effective combined force to combat modern-day piracy. ■

In 1868, the only dry dry docks in Hong Kong – Lamont and Hope – were in Aberdeen. [HK Museum of History]

Hong Kong in the early days, 1843. [Illustrated London News Picture Library]

CREATION OF A COLONY

HEALTH

It was not so much opposing armies, but disease, that became the real enemy facing troops and civilians as they struggled to establish themselves on Hong Kong Island. The scale of the problem is detailed in Captain Bernard's book, *Narrative of the Voyages and Services of the Nemesis*, published in 1844. Incidentally *Nemesis'* surgeon, Dr Young, left the ship to start the Hong Kong dispensary better known as 'Watsons'. The book had this to say about general health conditions:

Sickness had already begun to prevail among our troops before they had reached Hongkong [January 1841]. The eight days' exposure which they had endured upon the heights of Canton sowed the seeds of ague and dysentery which proved far more formidable enemies than any troops the Chinese could bring against us. After the lapse of a few days, and when the excitement of active operations on shore, and the cheering influence of hope and novelty

The Royal Naval Hospital, Wanchai, 1870s. The site, now occupied by Ruttonjee Sanatorium, is at the intersection of Kennedy Road and Queen's Road East. [Kathleen Harland]

had subsided, the sickness spread among the men with alarming rapidity, so that, at length, out of our small force, no less than 1100 men were upon the sick list at Hongkong. Part of this alarming state of things must be attributed certainly to the pernicious influence of the atmosphere of Hongkong itself at that season of the year. But every allowance must be made for the exposure which the men had undergone at Canton, and for the susceptibility of constitution produced by long confinement on board ship. The germs of disease were planted in their bodies before the men returned to the harbour of Hongkong, and therefore an undue stress was laid at the time upon the unhealthiness of Hongkong itself.

Disease having no respect for rank or station, the Senior Naval Officer of the time, Captain le Fleming Senhouse, fell victim to the prevailing sickness. At his own request, he was taken to Macau for burial in the Protestant cemetery. His grave is still there.

On 25th April 1841 the first naval Board of Inquiry was held in Hong Kong. The concern was the high death rate and measures which might be taken to reduce it. Medical science was insufficiently advanced to provide a solution. It is probable that most people were dying from malaria, transmitted through the *Anopheles* mosquito. The resulting fever,

though easily recognised, was not so easily treated with the medicines of the day. Originally, the cause of this fever was unscientifically attributed to unhealthy vapours coming through cracks in the ground. As a result, every effort was made to find a 'healthy spot' on the island.

Between May and October 1843, fever killed 24% of troops and 10% of civilians. Cramped living quarters for military personnel resulted in a higher mortality rate for troops. After this disastrous epidemic the Army barracks were moved from West Point to the Central district. *The Illustrated London News* of 8th November 1845 observed:

Its geology resembles that of the south of China – rotten rock, hard stiff clay, and red sandstone. On digging the foundations for buildings at Victoria a foul smell arose, caused by a gas which spreads sickness through the island. Its climate is variable, and, from its sudden transitions, dangerous to the health of its inhabitants. Situated on the verge of the tropics, there is a dry burning heat while the sun is approaching, and during the rainy monsoon a fearful pestiferous gas is emitted from the soil, which if it does not produce fever and speedy death, has the result of enervating both the body and mind. The Chinese look upon it as a 'fatal' island, and have left it to be habited by the refuse of their population. The climate produces the most weakening effects on the European constitution,

and few Englishmen can expect to live many years after residing there for some time.

General d'Aguilar, the first Commander of British Forces, commented in the same year, 'To retain Hongkong will require the loss of a whole regiment every three years, and to have 700 effective men, it is necessary to maintain 1400.'

The Navy had few, if any, quarters on land in the early days, and sailors were discouraged from going ashore too frequently in case they breathed 'bad air'. Whether conditions were any better on the hulks moored in the harbour is questionable, although it was certainly believed to be so at the time.

As a result of the poor health conditions it is not surprising that some of the first building projects on the island were naval and military hospitals. The structures were probably of the matshed type, quickly erected, and unfortunately, equally easily flattened. During the violent typhoon of 22nd July 1841, 'The over-crowded and badly built hospitals were all levelled to the ground and their fragments whirled through the air.'

The early colonists must have been very disheartened to have to literally pick up the pieces and start building again so soon after their first efforts. However, they learned their lesson and

Victoria from the north, c1865, artist unknown. [HK Museum of Art]

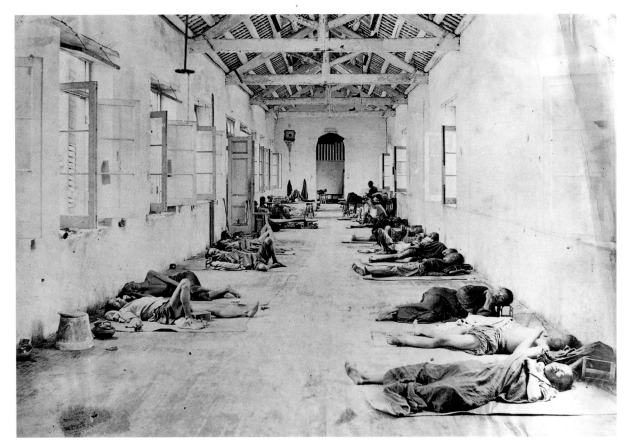

Bubonic Plague patients lie under the charge of a naval surgeon in a temporary hospital set up in a glass-works factory in Kennedy Town, 1894. [Public Records Office]

(1857-59), when the home authorities decided to increase the forces stationed permanently in Hong Kong. Consequently the supporting elements also had to be strengthened.

The increase in naval forces stationed in Hong Kong in the 1860s prompted the medical branch to agitate for its own hospital. It was wholly unsatisfactory to treat patients whilst swinging at anchor in mid-channel, let alone cope with the difficulties the typhoon season brought. Money was another problem.

The Seaman's Hospital had first opened in Wanchai in 1843 under the charge of Dr Young, and was backed financially by Jardine Matheson and Company. Patients were brought to the water-front hospital in this fashionable quarter by boat. It flourished, and provided many years of service to the community, but by the 1870s it was running at a loss. In 1873 *HMS Melville* was sold for HK$35,000 and the proceeds were spent in developing the hospital. Now far inland as a result of reclamation projects, a hospital still exists on this site at the junction of Kennedy Road and Queen's Road East.

In the event of disaster, naval doctors were always on call for the entire population of the colony. During the great Bubonic Plague of 1894, which killed thousands, a permanent Committee of the

subsequently used more substantial materials to construct buildings. Photographs show these have a remarkably solid air about them. The early Victorian philosophy of 'building to last' took on added significance in the typhoon-susceptible colony.

The Navy looked after its own sick. The original hospital ship that accompanied the fleet from Britain was *HMS Minden*. Later, in the 1840s, she was relieved by *HMS Alligator*, which in the 1860s was augmented by *HMS Melville*. A second hospital ship was required after the Second China War

Sanitary Board was set up, assisted by a naval surgeon, Dr Penny. The existing hospitals were filled to capacity, and special units were established onboard the *Hygeia* and at a glass-works factory that had recently been built but not fitted out. Chinese and western doctors working together under the supervision of Dr Penny sometimes found themselves dealing with 60 to 70 admissions a day.

An already difficult situation was worsened by widespread distrust of western medicine. This led many Chinese to conceal their sick and dying, furthering the spread of infection. In an attempt to combat this practice, the naval and military authorities, under Commodore Boyes and Major General Barker, were asked to initiate house-to-house searches. This tactic was effective from a health point of view, but aroused great public resentment. Demonstrations were held and placards appeared in the streets. Endeavouring to calm a dangerous situation, the Governor, Sir William Robinson, asked the Commodore to station a gunboat opposite the Tung Wah Hospital and Taipingshan. HMS *Tweed* was moved into position, but fortunately no further action was necessary.

Efforts were made to obtain the services of nursing sisters for the naval hospital, and at first it was hoped that they could be obtained from the

Aberdeen docks, destroyed by a typhoon in 1874. These docks were frequently used by naval vessels in the 19th century. [HK Museum of History]

civilian network. The Government Civil Hospital wrote in April 1895, saying that regrettably it had none to spare. The idea persisted, however, and in later correspondence to Vice Admiral Sir Alexander Buller, the Deputy Inspector wrote:

The benefits of nursing sisters have been so amply proved and the comfort and help they give to patients is so generally recognised that the Royal Naval Hospital here must be considered as being 'behind the times' without them. All the civilian hospitals in Hongkong are well provided with them, and they stand the climate as well as other people.

It was not until 1904 that nursing staff first arrived from the Queen Alexander's Royal Naval Nursing Service, members of which served continuously in the naval hospital until its closure in 1959. Three were working in the hospital when the Japanese attacked in 1941. Although it was bombed, 'between sixty and one hundred times', the three officers survived, and at the surrender they were transferred to the Stanley Internment Camp. They were released in August 1945 to take passage home on the hospital ship, *HMS Oxfordshire*.

When reorganisation took place at the end of WWII, the fabric of the building was discovered to have suffered considerably. Bombing, looting and neglect had left a shell that would have been more costly to resurrect than to start afresh elsewhere. Immediate service needs were met by taking over two floors of the Queen Mary Hospital, while the site of the new hospital was under discussion.

In November 1946 the War Memorial Hospital on the Peak (now commonly referred to as The Matilda Hospital) was taken over. Having been unoccupied for some time, it required considerable work. This was completed by 1948, and in January 1949 the Navy took possession of the new hospital with the transfer of all its patients from the Queen Mary. The hospital was used until 1959; thereafter naval patients were sent to the British Military Hospital, formerly situated on Bowen Road, and latterly on Wylie Road, Kowloon. Since 1995, with

The arrival of the Duke of Edinburgh in HMS Galatea (centre) in November 1869. Just to the right is Princess Charlotte. *The hospital ship in the left distance is probably HMS Melville sold in 1873 to pay for the new Royal Naval Hospital in Wanchai.*
[Public Records Office]

the closure of BMH, military and civilian doctors working in the Island Group Practice have looked after the health of Hong Kong Island servicemen and their families at the Prince of Wales Barracks.

EARLY SOCIAL LIFE

It is perhaps inevitable that the Navy should have had considerable impact on early colonial society.

The ratio of servicemen to civilians was much higher than today, and consequently any personalities or 'characters' among the naval personnel were easily noticed in a European population that was both inward-looking and homeward-orientated. A society that numbered billiard tables among its first imports and furnished its houses on the Peak in the latest London fashions would obviously defer to Her Majesty's representatives abroad.

The impact individual officers made is evident in the many place names with naval connections in modern-day Hong Kong. Mount Parker is named after Vice Admiral Sir William Parker; Kellett's Island and Mount Kellett commemorate another admiral of the 1870s; and Cochrane Street recalls the very popular Commander-in-Chief of the 1840s, Rear Admiral Sir Thomas Cochrane – who, it is recorded, entertained a great deal and was socially one of the best-known personages of his time.

Another feature of the early days were the public addresses presented to certain personages before going home. The Senior Naval Officer, Captain McQuhae, was the recipient of one such letter in 1848. Sir Michael Seymour in 1859 received not only an effusive address but also 2,000 guineas 'for services rendered and to show respect'. However, nothing at all was done for the Governor, Sir John Bowring, when he left a few weeks later! The best-documented of these addresses is, however, the first one, written to Captain Charles Talbot of *HMS Vestal* in 1847. The letter reads in part:

Having just learned with regret that you are about to take your immediate departure from China we hasten to express to you . . . how much we appreciate the kind consideration, the ready courtesy and the unremitting attention which you have ever displayed in your official capacity towards the mercantile community in China.

Cricket at Hong Kong, The Graphic, *26th August, 1876. [ILN Picture Library]*

This extract is indicative of the contribution the Navy made to the early domestic and social life of the colony. The merchants appreciated the Navy, whose guns afforded them shipping protection from pirates and the junks of the Chinese Emperor. Admiral Seymour was rewarded because he had vigorously prosecuted the 'Arrow War', which started when a Hong Kong-registered ship with a British captain was attacked while alongside at Canton.

Aside from fighting when necessary, the Navy made itself useful to the mercantile community in other ways. All the early surveys of the harbour and surrounding waters were performed by naval ships, among them *HM Ships Sulphur* and *Nassau*. Prior to the surveys, the China Sea was largely uncharted and was therefore considered dangerous for merchant shipping. Another service performed for the community was carrying mail between Hong Kong and the treaty ports in China, where merchants were permitted to pursue their trade.

The ceremony and pageantry which play such a part of naval routine would have added much colour to life in the colony. Edward H Cree, a naval surgeon serving in Hong Kong in 1845, recorded in his private journal:

14th February 1845. The navy got up a regatta. All the beauty and fashion of Hongkong onboard the Agincourt: about forty ladies and four times as many men. In the first race our second cutter pulled over the course, as none of the others would venture to compete with her. The race which excited most interest was one pulled by officers. After the racing, the prizes, consisting of purses of dollars, silver cups &c., which were distributed by the ladies on the poop of the Agincourt. At 6 dinner, but only half, about 140, could sit down at one time, although the table extended the whole length of the main deck. After dinner dancing occurred on the quarterdeck, which was prettily decorated with flags of all nations, chandeliers

The dockyard in 1878. The main entrance was between the two large buildings in the foreground which fronted Queen's Road. HMS Tamar can be seen to the left of Princess Charlotte *and* Victor Emmanuel, *her two predecessors as Receiving Ships. [Kathleen Harland].*

of bayonets, variegated lamps, transparencies and flowers. On the poop were card tables, &c. About 11 supper was served; afterwards dancing was kept up till 2 in the morning. Altogether the affair gave great satisfaction and will serve to bring the Hongkong people together. Everyone was asked, but one or two stuck-up ladies imagined themselves too good for the company, and stayed away, but they were not missed as they are old and ugly. The belles of the party were Miss Hickson and Miss Bowra.

Whether swinging down the *praya* (water-front road) on the way to exercise at Happy Valley, snapping to attention at a parade like that held in 1891 for the colony's 50th birthday, forming a guard of honour for a wreath-laying ceremony at the Cenotaph or putting on a show of illuminations as HMS *Tamar* did for the coronation of Edward VII in 1902, the Navy has been involved in much of the formal life of Hong Kong Island from the early days until the present.

DEVELOPMENT OF THE DOCKYARD

A Navy cannot operate without shore support for building, repairing, victualling and storing its sea-going fleet. The growing Far Eastern Fleet brought demand for such facilities, and the earliest reference to a naval yard in Hong Kong is probably that of a 22nd July 1856 memorandum from the Military to the Admiralty regarding the transfer of land for development. The area that became the first naval dockyard appears to be the section on which the Admiralty MTR station, south of Harcourt Road, and the current Prince of Wales Barracks, now stand.

Until 1959, the southern boundary of the dockyard was Queen's Road. Wellington Barracks was to the east and the North Barracks to the west. Part of the North Barracks had been acquired by the Navy in the 1850s. Between 1854 and 1856 the yard expanded at the expense of the North Barracks (used then by the artillery). In the Navy List for 1859, there is an entry for Hong Kong for the first time, under the heading, HM Victualling Yards. Thereafter, the dockyard and the victualling yard were listed as two separate establishments, each with

The landing of the Duke of Edinburgh at Pedder's Wharf, 2nd November 1869.
Pedder's Wharf was named after Lieutenant William Pedder of HMS Nemesis, *who in August 1841,*
became the Colony's first Harbour Master. [HK Museum of History]

its own officials. The dockyard officials were responsible for all the machinery and spare parts necessary to maintain and repair ships, whilst the victualling yard storekeepers would hold dry goods and foodstuffs. The expansion of the dockyard facilities, together with increased funding, resulted in the Dockyard Police replacing the old military guard in 1866.

Pedder's Wharf was the main landing stage for the entire waterfront. It was named after Lieutenant William Pedder of *HMS Nemesis* who, in August 1841, became the colony's first Harbour Master, Magistrate and Surveyor of Shipping. His office was on the slope to the east of Wyndham Street and his wharf was below, at the end of Pedder Street, the original waterfront.

The Harbour Master's Office, 1842. [Kathleen Harland]

A passage from the *Hongkong Telegraph* of 3rd September 1883 describes the wharf as:

> ... a miserably attenuated wooden structure. In size it is not one half large enough for the traffic of the city. From morning to night the flight of wooden steps are crowded with steam launches, men-of-war gigs and cutters ... and native craft of every description.

The acquisition of the Kowloon peninsula by Britain in January 1861 meant additional premises for the Navy. It is thought that a Royal Naval officer, Captain WK Hall of *HMS Calcutta*, was the first to appreciate the importance of the peninsula. He pointed out that the land would give much-needed sea frontage, and that Stonecutters Island could be useful as a quarantine area and for strengthening the defences of the island. He also suggested that the naval yard be moved to the mainland.

The then-Governor, Sir John Bowring, liked Hall's proposals and put them forward in his report to the Colonial Office. After Kowloon was ceded, a Board was set up to determine how the land was to be apportioned. The lion's share went to the Army, but the Navy acquired a site and used it for coal storage. The site remained naval property until 1959, when the entire yard was handed back to the civil authorities.

With two yards now in existence it was clear that more administrative posts had to be created commensurate with the increased responsibilities. In 1861 a Master Attendant of the Yard and an Accountant were appointed, and the Commander of the Receiving Ship (*HMS Princess Charlotte*) was made Naval Officer-in-Charge of the Naval Establishments. The post of Commodore-in-Charge Hong Kong was not created until five years later, and was to last for over a century, when it was replaced by that of Captain-in-Charge.

The post of Commodore was, however, reinstated in the summer of 1996 for the last year of the Territory's colonial rule.

In 1867, the Commodore asked the Surveyor General to measure the boundaries of the naval properties. This is detailed in correspondence of 1877 in which the Army claims that the Navy was encroaching on its property. Space in Central, even in the early days, was at a premium!

In 1880 an Inspector of Machinery was appointed for the first time. This old-fashioned-sounding title was changed to the more modern Chief Engineer in 1890. In 1884 the Inspector had under him a foreman, three engineers (for re-venting heavy guns), a boatswain and a carpenter. A year later they were joined by a constructor (for refits) and an Inspector of Shipwrights.

The particularly severe typhoon of 1874 caused extensive damage along the *praya*, and in 1875 discussions concerning new locations began. In his plans for reconstruction, the Governor, Sir Arthur Kennedy, suggested extending the *praya* eastwards in front of the naval and military areas. These areas, sloping down to the water, almost divided the colony in two, with Queen's Road the only link between the Central and Wanchai districts. The civil government was in favour of another

A. St. John's Cathedral (Protestant)   F. Albany   1. Victoria Peak, 1,825 feet above Sea   5. Siemssen and Co. Estab. 1848   8. Holliday, Wise, and Co. Estab. 1841   13. Lane, Crawford, and Co. Estab. 1850   18. Victoria Hotel—Donahoe and Hingkee
B. Mount Gough, 1,575 feet above Sea   G. Victoria Gap, 1,100 feet above Sea   2. High West, 1,774 feet above Sea   4. David Sassoon, Sons, and Co. Estab. 1841   9. Melchers and Co. Estab. 1866   14. Union Insurance Co. Estab. 1841   19. Arnhold, Karberg, and Co. Estab. 1866
C. Government House   H. High West, 1,774 feet above Sea   1. City Hall   5. Schellhass and Co. Estab. 1860   10. Hongkong Hotel   15. Douglas, Lapraik, and Co. Estab. 1841   20. Chinese Hongs
D. Clock Tower   I. St. Joseph's College   2. Hongkong and Shanghai Bank   6. W. R. Loxley and Co.   11. Jardine, Matheson, and Co. Estab. 1841   16. Wieler and Co. Estab. 1874   21. Peninsular and Oriental Steam Navigation Co.
E. College Gardens   K. Roman Catholic Cathedral   7. Russell and Co.   12. Siebuehlde and Hirst. Estab. 1855   17. Turner and Co.—Godowns   22. Chinese Hongs

PANORAMA OF THE TOWN OF VICTORIA, HONGKONG, AS SEEN FROM THE HARBOUR

WITH THE CHINA SQUADRON IN THE EAST—AT HONGKONG

Panorama of the town of Victoria, Hongkong, as seen from the harbour, The Graphic, *26th February 1887. [Wattis Fine Arts]*

connecting road, and the Navy did not object; the harbour was silting up in front of the yard, leaving their landing stage almost high and dry at low water. Sometimes stores had to be dragged in over a stretch of mud.

Kennedy hoped that the Admiralty would bear the cost, but the Admiralty felt that as the scheme would mainly benefit the civil sector, the colony should provide the funds. No more was heard on the subject, though the building of Kennedy Road, on the southern boundary of Victoria Barracks, did go through by way of a consolation prize to provide

a second major link with Wanchai. In 1885 the possibility of the *praya* being extended was quashed by the Admiralty's decision to extend the yard seawards through reclamation.

The first suggestion that the Navy should actually vacate its site was made in 1881 by Colonel Crossman RE, who wrote to the Governor proposing the transfer of the military and naval establishments to Causeway Bay. The Hong Kong Government would have been only too willing, but in March 1882 the Admiralty notified the Commander-in-Chief, Admiral Willes, that it could not agree.

Five years later, in March 1887, this time on the initiative of the civil government, a proposed move to land of equal value in Kowloon was considered. Although Commodore Morant was quite agreeable to the transfer, the Admiralty refused to purchase the land. Sir William des Voeux pleaded that for the civilian government to bear the transfer alone would involve the colony in 'ruinous expense', and so the proposal was shelved.

In 1896, the yard's southern boundary was redrawn to allow for the construction of what is now the east-bound carriageway of Queen's Road to

35

A close-up of dockyard buildings, the two piers in use with the sheers for bringing goods ashore, and launches from gunboats, which were moored in deeper water, c1880. [Royal Naval Museum]

Wanchai. At about the same time, the naval holdings expanded eastwards, swallowing up two rows of Chinese dwellings and shops.

On the opposite side of the naval base was the North Barracks, which the Navy had coveted for years as a solution to their growing accommodation needs. In addition, the living conditions onboard *HMS Victor Emmanuel* were becoming increasingly unhealthy. In 1887 the Navy acquired the North Barracks site and the Army was relocated. The yard was thus expanded to Murray Road, where it remained until the area was handed over to the government in 1959.

In May 1901, Commodore Powell forwarded to the Admiralty in London, Sir Paul Chater's proposal to move the base to the west side of the Kowloon peninsula. Sir Paul, a wealthy merchant and member of the Legislative Council, was the driving force behind the great reclamation scheme in Central that had begun in 1890. It extended the land from what is now Des Voeux Road (then the water-front road) to the present shoreline.

That October, the Admiralty rejected further plans to extend the reclamation along to Causeway Bay, and it was not until 1902 that the enormous undertaking of creating a brand new dockyard from the sea began.

AN EVENTFUL 1878

By 1878 the Navy was well established in the territory and had begun to exercise quite an influence on Hong Kong's day-to-day activities. In the same year, at the height of the Victorian era, *HMS Tamar* arrived in Hong Kong, and four huge fouled anchors were, for unknown reason, cast in iron in the gates of the dockyard. At the time, the naval year always began with the Victorian Rowing Regatta. Ships like the gunboats *Moorhen* and *Swinger* raced their gigs, while larger vessels such as *HMS Victor Emmanuel* used their whalers.

The ships in harbour at the beginning of 1878 were the Receiving Ship *HMS Victor Emmanuel*, flying the flag of Commodore Watson, its paddle dispatch boat *HMS Vigilant*, three gunboats; the *Lapwing*, *Curlew* and *Growler*, and *HMS Audacious*, the flagship of the China Squadron, which was paying its Christmas visit to the colony. At the end of January *HMS Tamar* returned from Singapore with the 74th Highlanders. Her officers were just in time to attend the Saturday night entertainment organised onboard *HMS Victor Emmanuel*, possibly in celebration of the Chinese New Year, which had just begun.

HMS Tamar *in 1877, when she served as a troop ship.* [Kathleen Harland]

The Naval Ball was held on 5th February at the City Hall in the presence of Governor and Mrs Hennessy. The bands of *HMS Audacious* and the 74th Highlanders provided the music. From a *Daily Press* reporter's description, it was obviously a memorable party:

The City Hall assumed a very gay appearance for the occasion, testifying to the hearty welcome of the gallant hosts. A field piece stood on each side of the hall; men-of-war's men lined the staircase and formed a guard of honour on arrival of the ladies; a Gatling gun occupied the centre of the first landing and was supported on each side by a boat gun and piles of polished projectiles. Two inflated diving dresses, more curious than ornamental, stood against the wall . . . a fountain embedded in

company, roaring out some rough sea-song in drunken chorus, or dancing to the time of a drum and flute, accordion or cornopean. The keepers of these grog-shops might be mistaken for respectable members of society were it not for their bull-dog, battered and damaged countenances, which betray sundry evidence of bruises and black eyes, received in taking the change out of their customers.

One such establishment was the infamous Beehive Inn. Its sign bore this verse:

Within this hive, we're all alive,
And pleasant is our honey:
If you are dry, step in and try,
We sell(s) for ready money.

As much as the Victorians enjoyed their night-time entertainment, with the light of day there were, of course, more serious matters for the Navy to address. On 19th February the Commander-in-Chief of the China Station, Vice Admiral Hillyar, took his flagship and four gunboats for tactical manoeuvring and target practice. Again the *Daily Press* was there to record the proceedings:

The Fleet exercised at general quarters during the day, firing at a rock distant about 2,800 yards and made excellent practice, all the shot falling within three feet of

Queen Victoria's Birthday Review, 26th May 1893. *[Public Records Office]*

rockwork played . . . while ferns and plants tastefully arranged and lighted by the ships lantern rendered the whole the delightful realisation of a happy thought.

At the other end of the social spectrum, life was also in full swing. The West Point Kennedy Town area then had the reputation among sailors as a good

'run-ashore'. A visitor to Hong Kong, Mr J Thomson, made these observations:

Passing west along Queen's Road, we came upon a quarter of the town much frequented by seamen of all nationalities. Here, spirits are sold in nearly every second shop and bands of sailors may be seen spending their time and money on questionable drink in more questionable

each other. At 11 p.m. the squadron exercised at night quarters, the guns being cast loose and three rounds were fired in three minutes. The 20th being very misty, the fleet remained at anchor in Tytam Bay. Yesterday morning at nine they weighed anchor and proceeding out of the bay they manoeuvred under steam and sail, the evolutions giving great satisfaction to the Admiral.

In March, Vice Admiral Hillyar stepped up the training programme for his crews in view of the political situation in Europe. Russia was at war with Turkey in an attempt to gain territorial concessions, and Britain and France were trying to intervene. Diplomatic overtures were achieving little and there was a possibility, albeit somewhat remote, that the China Squadron might have to repel a Russian attack from the north.

On 1st April it was announced that: 'In consequence of the war-like telegrams recently received we understand that all the munitions of war have been carefully surveyed.' Three days later, HMS Audacious, with Magpie in tow, left for a cruise 'under sealed orders'. A newspaper report from the time speculated that their final destination was an anchorage outside Vladivostock harbour, but subsequent reports place them no further north than Yokohama. The situation was viewed seriously

enough for HMS Victor Emmanuel to be moved from her mid-channel mooring to a station in front of the naval yard, '. . . for the protection of that establishment'.

Within a week, however, the excitement died down and Victor Emmanuel was back in her accustomed position. After all, even if there were to be a conflict, it would be unlikely to happen in Hong Kong waters. Nonetheless, several ships put in to refuel and re-provision on their way northwards, including the cruiser HMS Shannon and the composite corvettes HM Ships Diamond and Ruby.

May was another busy month for the Navy. In the Daily Press for 8th May there is what must be one of the earliest accounts of a torpedo trial in the East. The torpedo had been invented by Robert Whitehead, around 1866. The report states that the two used in this trial were manufactured at the Naval Yard – a certain tribute to its engineering capability. The account makes interesting reading:

Amongst the defensive measurements which have already been taken and are at present being prosecuted for the protection of the Colony is that of the manufacture of torpedoes at the Naval Yard. For some time past a number of these machines have been in the course of construction, between seventy and eighty being now ready for use, and

yesterday an experiment was tried in the Ly-ee-moon Pass, with the double object of showing its effectiveness and giving the men a little torpedo practice. . .

The junk to be destroyed was towed out in the Pass just this side of Shaujiwan. The pinnace steamed slowly towards her, but it was evident there was some hitch, for when the firing line was pulled there was no result; another and another attempt was made, and yet no blow up. It was then discovered, on more closely examining the drum, that the firing key was broken, and that the water had got in. Luckily, two torpedoes were shipped and immediately the attempt was made with the second one, up went the junk in a thousand pieces and a large column of water at least forty feet high, and although the pinnace went hard astern, she did not clear the radius of the falling water and timbers of the junk soon enough to escape a drenching, and one piece of timber striking Lieutenant Needham on the back, he was knocked overboard and sucked down to some depth, but as he received no injury from the blow, he was soon able to strike out and get on board again.

The experiment was a great success in as much that it showed that a steam launch could emerge from a creek and in a few minutes explode one of these torpedoes under the broadside of an enemy's ship. An ironclad could not withstand such an explosion without being destroyed or totally disabled.

Torpedo classroom in Hong Kong dockyard, late 19th century. [Officers' Mess POWB, Royal Naval Museum]

The experiment was witnessed by His Excellency the Governor and Commodore Watson, and a large number of naval and military men and public. The arrangements were under the supervision of Lieutenant Needham, of Victor Emmanuel, *as torpedo officer, and concluded about six when quite a flotilla of steam launches returned to Hongkong.*

Another grand spectacle for the people of Hong Kong came a few weeks later on 28th May, Queen Victoria's official birthday. All men-of-war in harbour dressed ship, and at noon royal salutes were fired from *Victor Emmanuel* and the shore battery, probably Wellington Barracks. In fact, this was just one of the many official salutes of the year. George Washington's birthday, the anniversary of the Queen's accession, the anniversary of her coronation and the birthdays of the Prince of Wales and the King of Spain, were all accorded the same recognition.

On the political scene there was still no sign of action against the Russians, and by September the ships began to return from the north. The ironclad, *HMS Iron Duke*, had come out to relieve *HMS Audacious* as the Admiral's flagship in October, and there was the usual leave-taking ceremony.

As *HMS Audacious* steamed slowly through the men-of-war anchorage with Vice Admiral Hillyar onboard, she was loudly cheered by sailors on the rigging of *Victor Emmanuel* and the gunboats, while Portuguese, American and Russian ships joined in. However, the German gunboat, *Freya*, 'was conspicuous by her crew remaining below'.

The year ended in a vein similar to that in which it had begun, with home-made entertainment on-board *HMS Victor Emmanuel* and the traditional Victorian Regatta:

Commodore Watson laid on some 'negro entertainment' for his guests, by courtesy of crew members of Magpie. *The programme consisted of minstrelsy and a well-known sketch entitled 'The Barber's Shop'. As ever, the evening passed off well, much appreciated by a joint naval/army audience, leavened by the presence of several ladies.*

THE NAVY IN THE NEW TERRITORIES

In 1898 the Hong Kong Government took over, on a 99-year lease, a further section of the Kowloon mainland known as The New Territories, primarily for defence. China was in a weakened state at the time and this had enabled Germany, France and Russia to obtain territorial concessions. Fearing that any further acquisitions by these countries would threaten British interests in the area, the British Government determined to enlarge the size of the colony. China agreed to lease 355 square miles, extending from Deep Bay and Mirs Bay in the north, to Lamma Island in the south.

The transaction was not without incident. There were, among the Chinese, those who felt a sense of mistrust, and the Navy was called upon to play a mainly supportive peace-keeping role. At midnight on 3rd April 1898, the governor, Sir Henry Blake, sent a hurried note to the Senior Naval Officer, Commodore Powell, asking for one of Her Majesty's Ships to convey about 100 soldiers to Pai Po Hu (the modern Tai Po). There, the Civil Secretary, six Sikh policemen and 10 Chinese 'braves' were holding out against a 'threatening mob'. *HMS Whiting* sailed at 0330, with the Commander of British Forces, General Gascoigne, onboard. Bringing up the rear was *HMS Fame*, serving as dispatch vessel, and two gunboats.

Unfortunately, on the way to Mirs Bay, *HMS Whiting* suffered some damage when it struck a shoal. In a letter to the Commodore, General Gascoigne sportingly pointed out that the vessel had been asked to proceed with all speed, and that the mishap

Chinese Torpedo Whaler crew with a dockyard gardener c1880. [Officers' Mess POWB]

Trouble of a more serious nature did, however, develop a few days later in the same area. About 1,000 uniformed Chinese gathered on the hills round Pai Po Hu and began to fire down into the camp of the recently reinforced Hong Kong Regiment. *HMS Fame*, again ordered up in support, opened fire with its 11-pounder guns, silencing the Chinese battery. Lieutenant Keys landed with a party of men and helped the troops clear the hills. The incident was serious enough to make the Governor decide that the Union Jack should be raised a day earlier than planned, so that when the territory passed into British possession, he could act freely against any Chinese malcontents.

On 16th April, the General, the Commodore and Mr Lockhart (the Colonial Secretary) proceeded in *HMS Brisk* to Pai Po Hu, where the ceremony was performed without opposition. The Governor wished the flag to be shown also in Kowloon City, and *HMS Peacock* was towed there (not having had time to raise steam) to fire a salute.

The final incident of the 'campaign' took place on the border in May. General Gascoigne asked Commodore Powell for naval assistance in the occupation of Sum Chun. This took the form of a naval brigade commanded by Captain Clarke of *HMS Undaunted*: there were 100 bluejackets and 30

seemed unavoidable. The Commodore's comments are unrecorded!

The vessels arrived at Tolo harbour in Mirs Bay at 0900 and the troops were disembarked. The situation was less serious than had been anticipated;

a matshed had been burnt down, but the Civil Secretary had been allowed to leave in safety. The General, seeing no reason for the troops to remain, signalled at 1330 for the boats to pick up the men and everyone was home in time for tea.

Torpedo boats, power base of the Navy in Hong Kong during the late 19th century.
[Officers' Mess POWB]

Mobilisation of Kowloon-based torpedo boats to fight pirates in the South China Sea, 1873.
[Officers' Mess POWB]

marines from his own ship, the same from *HMS Aurora*, and 30 marines from *HMS Tamar*. They sailed in the *Swift* and the *Firebrand* to Starling Inlet, where they disembarked and marched inland to meet converging columns from Pai Po Hu and Deep Bay. The Union Jack was hoisted at Sum Chun and a 21-gun salute fired. No Chinese were to be seen. The following morning the troops and ships departed, everyone satisfied that the right sort of demonstration had been made.

Although these series of events probably seem unimportant – given the lack of action and sense of anti-climax – the Chinese dissidents were real enough. That they did not make their presence felt, was, in all likelihood, due to the prompt action of the civil and service authorities and to the efficiency with which their orders were carried out. Commodore Powell commented: 'The question of pacifying the newly acquired territory is a military one and should be left to the troops as much as possible.' However, the Secretary of State for the Colonies in Britain paid tribute to the naval forces: 'I have pleasure in bringing to the notice of the Lords Commissioners of the Admiralty the prompt and efficient services rendered by naval officers trusted with the transport of troops.'

The New Territories are now of significant industrial importance to Hong Kong. The water supply to island island flows through it, and it also provides valuable land in a colony hard-pressed for space. The expiry of the lease in 1997 was never going to be a problem to those who secured it at the turn of the century, and neither could they have foreseen that it would become inextricably linked to the eventual return of Hong Kong to China through fulfillment of the Joint Declaration of 1984.

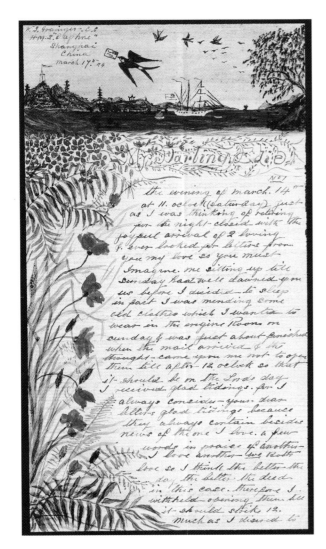

Three of the 174 letters Chief Stoker Walter Grainger wrote to his fiancée, Edith Townsend, between 1895 and 1901.
This period included his three years in HMS Daphne on the China Station. [The Royal Naval Museum]

THE NEW DOCKYARD

At the turn of the century the Navy was still faced with the problem of how to create the space necessary for a modern dockyard. Since the only possible direction was seawards, the decision was taken to carry through a massive reclamation scheme before, and alongside the building programme. One consequence was a further increase in engineering personnel.

The area finally created covered over 39 acres. The new sea walls, 4,580 feet long, were designed as deep water quay walls. They could bear the weight of large guns, boilers and cranes, and formed a bulwark against the sea. Two novel features were a floating basin and a graving, or dry-dock. Designed to have an area of over 9 acres and a depth, at the lowest spring tides, of 30 feet, the square-shaped basin was used to repair and refit vessels while they were still afloat. The dry-dock was 550 feet long and its lowest depth was also 30 feet. It was large enough to dry-dock the aircraft carrier *HMS Hermes*, which was stationed in Hong Kong between the two world wars, and was also capable of taking three submarines at one time.

This massive project undoubtedly posed

The recently completed naval dockyard c1905. [HK Museum of History]

technical problems. Much of the work had to be done underwater, and the walls had to be completed to four-fifths of their height before they were even visible. This involved training about 20 local Chinese divers, who proved to be skilful workers.

The preparation of the materials was also no mean task. The contractors established a huge depot at Mataukok in Kowloon Bay, where they manufactured the concrete blocks with which the sea wall was to be built. This site was chosen

Hosts and Guests captures a gathering of ships from Britain, France and Russia, 1897.
[Kathleen Harland]

pumps and boilers, as well as two pairs of 15-feet Invincible series centrifugal pumps driven by vertical compound condensing engines that could lift several thousand gallons per minute from a depth of 62 feet.

By the time the ceremonial foundation stone was laid on 15th January 1902, about half the work of dredging the floating basin, one-third of the excavations for the graving dock and four-fifths of the foundation work for the quay walls had been completed. The event marked the culmination of a great deal of work and planning, and signalled that for the foreseeable future, the Navy would remain at the heart of the rapidly expanding city. The ceremony attracted much public attention at the time, and was well reported by the local press. Mrs Powell, wife of the Commodore, officially placed the stone. Despite the general sycophancy of the age, not all were overjoyed. The *China Mail* for 14th January commented:

It is one of the most obvious proofs that Hong Kong exists primarily as a naval and military base that the wishes of the Colonial Government and the commercial community of the Colony have had the least weight in the decision arrived at respecting the position of the Dockyard and the form the alterations should take.

because of an ample supply of granite. Even then, a huge reclamation scheme had to be carried out before the block yard and pier, from which the stone was sent across the harbour, could be built.

A large quantity of plant also had to be provided, much of it specially designed. The dredger *St Enoch* was a powerful vessel for those days, capable of carrying 600 tons of spoil from a depth of 46 feet.

She lifted the hard material from the future basin at the rate of about 1,800 tons a day, most of which, of course, was simply moved across the site to the proposed land area. Other machinery consisted of four steam pile-drivers, four locomotives, six portable cranes, three 10-ton cranes on barges for settling the blocks, and numerous wagons and trolleys. The dry-dock, built behind a coffer dam, had its own

Interestingly the memorial stone laid at this time was found in October 1959, when the dry-dock was being filled in under the dockyard closure scheme. The *China Mail* for 1st October that year reported:

The copy of the China Mail *dated January 14th, 1902 and of the* Hongkong Daily Press *the day after, six coins ranging from a dollar to a cent and a faded plan showing the extent of the Dockyard extension being undertaken at the time the stone was laid, were in a glass container found under the memorial stone at the head of the dock. The memorial stone and the relics are being retained by the Naval Yard Authorities pending Admiralty instructions.*

The glass container was opened in 1959 and its contents resealed in 1962 with similar artefacts from that year. This new time capsule was reburied under the original memorial stone in a small garden in the naval base. On the 15th January 1997, exactly 95 years after the original burial, Mrs Janet Melson, wife of the Commodore, opened it again, and the memorabilia of the heyday of the empire were finally consigned to the military museum at Lei Yue Mun, pending the arrival of the People's Liberation Army of China into the base that had, for so long, been synonymous with the Royal Navy. ◼

Torpedo workshop personnel, Kowloon, 1898. [Officers' Mess POWB]

The French destroyer Fronde *following the typhoon of 18th September 1906.*
[Public Records Office]

HMS Phoenix *after the typhoon of 18th September 1906.* [Public Records Office]

HMS Powerful *coaling. Tamar is in the background. At the height of the Empire in 1898, the Royal Navy was never far from a British port with docks, coaling stations and naval bases.* [Lieutenant Commander Charles Addis and FormAsia Books Ltd]

A group of officers on coaling duty in 1898. [Lieutenant Commander Charles Addis and FormAsia Books Ltd]

ESTABLISHMENT AND EMPIRE

A NAVAL BUILD-UP

The build-up of the Royal Navy in the China Station, for which the new dockyard had been built, continued apace until war began to loom in Europe. In the last decade of the 19th century the fleet expanded, until by 1900 three battleships, 15 cruisers, six sloops, 10 gunboats, five shallow-draught river steamers, six torpedo boat destroyers, a store ship and a despatch vessel were based in Hong Kong. By 1905 the number of destroyers had doubled and the fleet remained at this size until the outbreak of the First World War. To accommodate this fleet, and after protracted negotiations, the Navy acquired more land from the Army, which withdrew entirely from North Barracks and Wellington Barracks, and ceded all the land north of Queen's Road.

The First World War affected Hong Kong only from a distance. The Japanese remained allies and the colony faced no immediate threat. The real risk

The dockyard photographed at the start of the First World War. The buildings in the left-hand corner were built in the original area owned by the Navy. To the north lies reclaimed land. To the right is Wellington Barracks, taken over in 1946 by the Navy.
[Public Records Office]

Impressive naval and military parades down Chater Road formed the centrepiece of Hong Kong's programme of celebrations marking the coronation of George V in 1911. As Prince George, the monarch had visited the colony in 1881 with his brother Prince Albert, when both were midshipmen in HMS Bacchante. [FormAsia Books Ltd]

Seamen from HMS Marazion hoisting a 21" torpedo following a trial firing by submarine L9.
[Lieutenant David Grey RN]

At the end of the War, HMS Terrible staged a patriotic salute – the lettering formed entirely
by sailors in the ship. Hong Kong had shared the anguish of its allies at war, and when
the Armistice came the city rejoiced. [HMS Tamar]

came from the possibility of a German victory and the consequent loss of Hong Kong to Germany. It was not surprising, therefore, that the bulk of Hong Kong's forces were withdrawn at the outbreak of war, leaving defence of the colony essentially to volunteer forces.

The only part the Navy played in the First World War in Hong Kong was as a signal station. A contemporary order by the Governor had stated: 'In the event of hostile vessels being sighted three guns will be fired from *Tamar* and the red British

Ensign hoisted on that vessel [*Tamar*] and at the masthead of the flagstaff on the Peak, and will be kept hoisted as long as the enemy is in sight.' There is no record of the Red Ensign having been hoisted, either in *Tamar* or ashore, during the First World War.

On 6th August 1914, all German residents were arrested and interned at Stonecutters Island. Shortly afterwards *HMS Triumph* sailed to join the fleet at Tsing-Tao with the 2nd Battalion Duke of Cornwall's Light Infantry embarked. On passage,

she intercepted the German steamer *Hanametal* and took her into Wei-Hai-Wei with a prize crew on board. The next day she did the same with the Hamburg-Amerika Line ship, *Frisia*. This proved a fortuitous capture as, on 25th August, the 2nd Battalion was ordered to France and returned to Hong Kong in the *Frisia* without further delaying *HMS Triumph*. Tragically, by April 1915 the Battalion had lost all of its officers except one in the first battle of Ypres.

As the conflict in Europe escalated, young sailors prepared to leave their Far East base for distant battlegrounds. [FormAsia Books Ltd]

Hong Kong's dockyards were the most sophisticated in the East. HMS Hawkins is seen here undergoing refit at the Taikoo Dockyards in Kowloon, 1921. [Hong Kong United Dockyards Ltd / FormAsia Books Ltd]

The Hawkins Bowl, an Officers' Mess trophy from the Prince of Wales Barracks. Presented to the ship by the Hongkong and Shanghai Banking Corporation, the Bowl is in remembrance of the gallant and invaluable services rendered to the bank at Yokohama in September 1923.

Marazion's piper, Petty Officer J Baxter, 1921. [Lieutenant David Grey RN]

HMS Marazion in dry dock in the naval dockyard, 1921. [Lieutenant David Grey RN]

HM Submarine L9, stationed in Hong Kong, but lost in a typhoon of 1923.
[Lieutenant David Grey RN]

Admiral Sir AL Duff, C-in-C China Station inspecting a naval brigade
at Wei-Hai-Wei, on Coronation Day, 22nd June 1921.
[Lieutenant David Grey RN]

Piracy continued to plague the colony well into the 20th century. This picture, taken onboard SS Ostend in 1927, shows a naval anti-piracy squad with their mannacled prisoners who had been captured after taking China Navigation Company Steamer Sunning – an ill-fated ship that was pirated twice and finally wrecked in Junk Bay during a typhoon. [John Swire and Sons]

HEYDAY OF THE CHINA STATION

The period between the two World Wars was probably the heyday of the Royal Navy's China Station. The fleet based in Hong Kong consisted of the 5th Cruiser Squadron, one ship of which flew the flag of the Commander-in-Chief, China Station; the 4th Submarine Flotilla of 12 boats; the Yangtse Flotilla of 10 gunboats, and the West River Flotilla of five; the 8th Destroyer Flotilla of nine ships and usually an aircraft carrier – frequently *HMS Hermes*.

The large number of gunboats based in Hong Kong was in response to the extended civil wars in China, where British interests and citizens were threatened initially by local warlords and pirates, then by the fervour of the Nationalists and the Communists, and finally by the Japanese. There were violent anti-foreign outbursts at Canton, Hangkow, Nanking and Shanghai from the mid to late 1920s. Frequently, larger warships were deployed from Hong Kong and Wai-Hei-Wei to restore order.

In 1937, as the Japanese invaded Manchuria and then China itself, the Royal Navy became involved in the large-scale evacuation of British citizens from Shanghai to Hong Kong. The Japanese bombed and

(Above) Holy stoning the decks of a warship. A combination of sand, water and a great deal of elbow grease kept the wooden decks clean.
[Kathleen Harland]

(Left) Washing down after coaling. Maintaining a vessel in a seaworthy condition in the days of steam was no easy matter.
[Kathleen Harland]

HRH The Prince of Wales received an impressive welcome when he landed at Hong Kong on 7th April 1922. Here, he is seen taking the formal salute before departing by sedan chair.
[Public Records Office]

shelled its ships. By 1939 the British concession at Tientsin was threatened and the experience gained there, in trying to maintain a foothold in China, weighed heavily on British strategic decisions in the defence of Hong Kong when Japan entered the Second World War. ▪

A naval party landing at Bias Bay, 1927; a notorious base for pirates. [HK Museum of History]

The recovery of Lieutenant Renwick's aircraft, on 4th April 1927. [HK Museum of History]

Submarine HMS Proteus passing Kowloon in 1932. [Public Records Office]

A Royal Navy wedding when Pamela Poland, daughter of Captain Allan Poland, the Commanding Officer of HMS Medway, and Commander CT Addis were married at St John's Cathedral in 1933. Their son, Charles Addis became Flag Lieutenant to the Commodore-in-Charge in 1958. [Lieutenant Commander CP Addis RN / FormAsia Books Ltd]

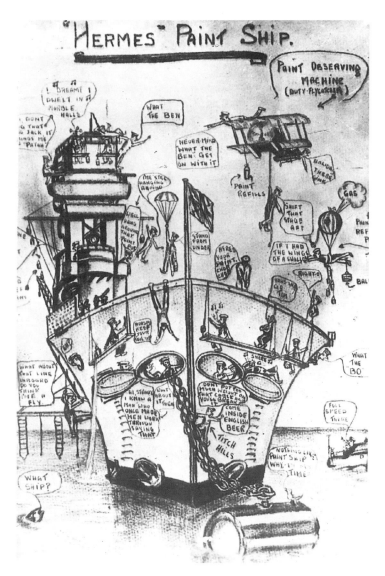

The crew of HMS Hermes *as they saw themselves in the Fragrant Harbour.*
[Public Records Office]

HMS Hermes *frequently visited Hong Kong between the two world wars.*
The photograph, together with a cartoon from the ship's line book, shows her
moored in Victoria Harbour. [Public Records Office]

(Following page) A good example of military aid to the local community:
a naval party helping put out a fire in a building at the junction of Des Voeux
Road Central and Chater Road in the 1930s. [Public Records Office]

SURRENDER AND SWIFTSURE

UNAVOIDABLE CONFLICT

Since 1939, Britain had been fighting a bitter and bloody war. Hong Kong was becoming increasingly isolated from Europe, and it had been clear for a long time that its defence would be limited. Good strategic reasons existed for choosing Singapore rather than Hong Kong as the British Far Eastern base. A cruiser squadron operating from there could, within two days, be either in the Indian Ocean or off the southern coast of China. Singapore lay at the end of a peninsula that was also British territory, and was protected by a solid bloc of British, Dutch and French possessions; only the independent Kingdom of Siam (Thailand) was identified as a likely jumping-off ground for Japanese aggression. Hong Kong, on the other hand, although well situated for action in the China Sea, was uncomfortably close to Japan.

The Japanese occupation of China and Taiwan meant that Hong Kong was vulnerable to attack and capture at any time. Reinforcement was therefore not part of any defence plan. As the British Prime Minister Winston Churchill minuted in 1941, 'There is not the slightest chance of holding Hong Kong or relieving it. It is most unwise to increase the loss we shall suffer there.'

However Major-General Grassett, former General Officer Commanding (GOC) Hong Kong persuaded Churchill that by reinforcing Hong Kong the defending forces would be able to hold out for considerably longer – enough perhaps, for the war in Europe to have ended. Churchill agreed and two Canadian battalions were deployed to Hong Kong in November 1941.

In December, Hong Kong's own forces consisted of both regulars and volunteers from all three services, conscription having been introduced in 1939 for men aged 18 to 41. In addition, many European and Commonwealth nationals had signed up for the volunteer defence forces. So did many

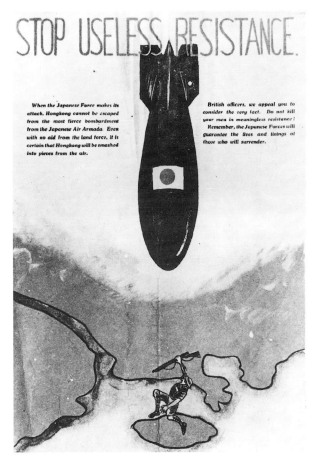

A Japanese propaganda leaflet dropped over Hong Kong prior to its surrender on Christmas Day 1941. [Kathleen Harland]

61

Chinese, although they were unarmed and served as drivers, orderlies and medics.

Naval forces consisted of approximately 1,600 Royal Navy, Royal Marines and Hong Kong Royal Naval Volunteer Reserve (HKRNVR) personnel. Since there would be no serious naval defence of Hong Kong, two of the three destroyers were ordered to Singapore on the evening of 8th December, the first day of the Japanese invasion. Among the remaining naval forces, however, something of the Nelsonian spirit was in evidence, aptly epitomised in Lieutenant Commander Boldero, the one-armed Captain of *HMS Cicala*: his was the last ship to be put out of action in Hong Kong.

THE BATTLE FOR HONG KONG, 1941

The Japanese attack on Hong Kong commenced at approximately 0800 hours on 8th December 1941, a few hours after it attacked Malaya and Pearl Harbour. Even though garrison troops had demolished key crossing points the day before, the Japanese crossed the border into the New Territories using barges and pontoon bridges. Commander FW

The Motor Torpedo Boat Flotilla, a rather grand name for six old craft, the final line of naval resistance. [Colin Aitchison]

Crowther kept an account of the period. He wrote:

On December 8th at about 5.30 am I was rung up in my house in the dockyard and told the war had started. The Japanese troops had crossed the frontier on the mainland of Hong Kong territory, that is on the Kowloon side. After informing all concerned on the telephone we immediately started everything going according to plan. At 8 am the Japanese sent over about fifty aeroplanes and strafed Kai Tak aerodrome, and all our planes (5 small out-of-date ones) were destroyed, and then we had none at all. Our naval force consisted of three destroyers, two of which were ordered to Singapore, and left that night, so then we only had one, the Thracian. In addition we had one fair sized gunboat (HMS Cicala) available and two small ones, and eight motor torpedo boats. That is all the real fighting navy we had, but in addition we had some small armed merchant vessels called APV's (Auxiliary Patrol Vessels) manned by HKRNVR officers with Chinese crews which were useless as fighting units and used purely for patrol purposes . . . So the battle became a purely land affair and most of the naval personnel were employed as soldiers.

In fact the Navy played several other roles in the defence of Hong Kong. They gave fire support to land forces; intercepted Japanese landing craft attempting to cross the harbour; moved troops to new strategic locations; evacuated troops; and finally, when all else had failed, saw to the destruction of shipping too valuable to be allowed to fall into enemy hands. In particular *HM Ships Robin, Tern, Aldgate, Barlight* and *RFA Ebonol* were all scuttled.

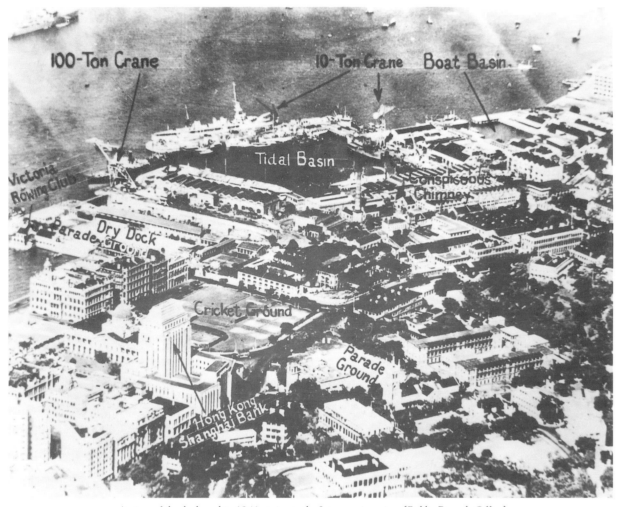

100-Ton Crane
10-Ton Crane
Boat Basin
Tidal Basin
Victoria Rowing Club
Conspicuous Chimney
Dry Dock
Parade Ground
Cricket Ground
Parade Ground
Hong Kong Shanghai Bank

A view of the dockyard in 1941, prior to the Japanese invasion. [Public Records Office]

At this time 47 Royal Marines were serving at *HMS Tamar*, under command of Lieutenant Colonel Robert Giles RM. The marines and naval personnel were deployed to reinforce land forces and records show that Colonel Giles instructed his marines to assist with the defence of the island ' . . . to the last man and last round.'

The Army was deployed on both the mainland and the island. The Mainland Brigade was deployed along what was known as Gin Drinkers Line, an 18-kilometre stretch of fortifications starting at Gin Drinkers Bay in the west and winding its way through the New Territories to Port Shelter in the east. Built in the mid 1930s in response to possible Japanese invasion after the fall of Canton, in 1938 the Army felt that the line was not defendable with the troops available. Policy therefore focused on protecting Hong Kong Island by building batteries and pill boxes along the shoreline and on high ground. With the Canadian reinforcements, however, Gin Drinkers Line once again became central to the defence of Hong Kong.

At a crucial part of the line, at Smugglers Ridge, was Shing Mun Redoubt, a large citadel guarding the most vulnerable route into Kowloon. Although in a poor state of repair, it was designed to be defended by at least 100 men. On 8th December, only a 30-man platoon and 'A' Company HQ of the Royal Scots held the citadel. By evening the Japanese had taken up high ground overlooking Gin Drinkers Line and the next evening the infantry attack commenced. Fierce opposition from the defending troops ensued, but by the morning of the 10th, those remaining gave orders to the batteries on Stonecutter's Island to shell Shing Mun Redoubt

On 8th December 1941, Japanese planes initially attempted to bomb the colony into submission.
On 18th December the Japanese invaded the island and finally took control on Christmas Day.
[FormAsia Books Ltd]

The dockyard, a primary target, under attack.
[FormAsia Books Ltd]

as it finally fell into Japanese hands.

The fall of the Shing Mun Redoubt in fewer than two days – in contrast to expectations of it being held for 7 to 14 days – was perhaps the most crucial loss in the early stages of the invasion, effectively opening up Kowloon to the Japanese. On the evening of 11th December the Mainland Brigade withdrew to Hong Kong Island under covering fire from Stonecutter's Island. This was the last action conducted from Stonecutter's; the guns and positions were destroyed and abandoned later that night.

Between the 11th and 13th of December the Navy carried out a miniature Dunkirk. HMS *Thracian* was instrumental in evacuating the 5/7 Rajputs from the Devil's Peak area, coming in as close as her captain, Lieutenant Commander Pears, dared. Shells and mortar bombs exploded around the troops as they waded out to the ships which then took them to Aberdeen. Commander Crowther wrote:

On the night of the 11th-12th, we evacuated our troops and their stores from the mainland to Hong Kong island, the Japs occupying Kowloon on the 12th … we could easily see them across the harbour, about 1100 yards away, and sometimes, they even potted at us with rifles. They now shelled us in earnest. One morning in a little under an hour, we counted about 230 shells falling in the

dockyard … It was, however, extraordinary how few casualties we had when walking about the dockyard. We also had a lot of trouble from the fifth column snipers potting at us from houses in the town behind.

After withdrawing to Hong Kong Island, the forces were reorganised and deployed across the island in two brigades. For the next five days the Japanese shelled the island almost continually. They also dropped propaganda leaflets and made radio broadcasts to lower morale amongst the civilian population. Commander Crowther continued:

I did not leave the dockyard as I expected a frontal attack across the harbour at any time, particularly at night… apart from the defences in the yard we were fully employed putting the fires out which were caused by shells and bombs. We were usually shelled whilst doing this and on one occasion they got a direct hit with a shell on the fire engine, seriously wounding two of our men, both of whom are miraculously still alive and practically all right now. Although I was only about five yards away at the time, I did not get a scratch … We only had one or two actually killed.

The old Tamar, the wooden depot ship, [had been] taken out of the dockyard on the 8th December and we sank her at her buoy on the 12th. We also destroyed all confidential matter not actually in use on the 12th. On

Resultant damage to the dockyard. December 1941. [FormAsia Books Ltd]

the 13th Dec the few troops we had on Devil's Peak Peninsula were taken to the island of Hong Kong, and then the Japs had complete control of the mainland which put them only 800 yards off the island.

On 13th December a Japanese officer with three female European hostages crossed the harbour under a white flag of truce and offered negotiations for the surrender of Hong Kong. That offer was refused, as well as one on the 17th.

Having established themselves on the mainland, the Japanese attempted to cross the harbour on the night of 15th December. Warned by the shore batteries on the north side, HMS *Thracian* sailed from Aberdeen into Kowloon Bay, darkness providing sufficient cover against the enemy guns. The need to keep close to the shore, however, necessitated running some risks and the ship ran aground, causing flooding to her forward compartment. Commander Crowther recorded the developments:

Our only destroyer, the Thracian, was grounded at Uk Kok when going into harbour at night to attack some junks full of Jap troops, but although badly damaged, managed to get off quickly and destroyed the junks. I sent Lieutenant Cole RN to look after Aberdeen dockyard as I expected the Japs to attack our dockyard at Hong Kong

at any time, which they could have done easily . . . That evening, at sunset, the Thracian was docked at Aberdeen. On the 16th at 1330 hours there was a very accurate high level bombing attack on Aberdeen dockyard, apparently after the Thracian. Big fires were started and there were many casualties. Lieutenant Cole was killed. The Thracian had a near miss, killing a few, but she herself was not seriously damaged. As it was found that the damage suffered by the Thracian when grounding was greater than could be repaired at Aberdeen all her armament etc. was removed and at 0530 on the 17th she was undocked and steamed to a nearby island [Round Island] where she was run aground and abandoned. Then we had no destroyer . . .

On the night of 18th December the Japanese landed along the north coast at three main points between North Point and Lye Mun. Crowther continued:

On the 18th after a heavy bombardment the Japs landed at about 2100 on North Point and Taikoo dockyard and were in the centre of the island by daybreak having annihilated all opposition. Whenever they were stopped by our troops they simply streamed past on both flanks and surrounded our men. The guns that could bear on the boats crossing the harbour were soon put out of action.

Commodore AC Collinson ordered five motor torpedo boats (three of which were commanded by members of the HKRNVR) to attack. The Japanese guns and aircraft were too much and these craft were all sunk, but not before they destroyed a number of Japanese troop-carriers in the harbour.

The end was in sight. The Navy was increasingly forced to fight on land as its vessels were destroyed. Many naval personnel had, however, been fighting on land since the invasion began. HMS *Cicala*, which had been engaged in the melancholy task of sinking merchant ships, was the last ship to be put out of action on 20th December, again through air attack. Her crew, however, managed to escape and four hours later were fighting as soldiers around Benett's Hill in the west of the island. The Industrial School at Aberdeen became the new headquarters from where naval parties joined the Army in the fight for Stanley and Repulse Bay. Many naval personnel fought and died alongside their Army comrades.

One expedition in particular, on 19th December, saw a party of 30 ratings from HMS *Thracian* sent out to reinforce Brigadier Lawson's HQ at Wong Nei Chong Gap, which was being defended by members of the Winnipeg Grenadiers and the Hong Kong Volunteer Defence Corps. A company of Royal Scots had been sent from Wanchai earlier but had been attacked en route and most of them had been killed. The naval party were also ambushed, but survivors managed to escape to a nearby house, Postbridge, south of the Gap. After holing up for several hours they came out bearing the white flag of truce. Three were immediately bayoneted. Able Seaman Ronald Mattieson, seeing the fate of his shipmates, struck the rifle out of the hand of an advancing Japanese soldier and dived headlong over the cliff, rolling and tumbling to the beach, where he found a small cave which became his home for the next month. At the price of a broken collar bone he had saved his life.

Meanwhile, the last of the defenders at the Gap, with the few Royal Scots survivors, were surrounded. Lawson's last radio broadcast summed up the brave spirit of these men: 'They're all around us, I'm going outside to shoot it out.' They were all killed. Brigadier Lawson was the highest ranking officer to be killed in the battle for Hong Kong. Commander Crowther observed:

On the 19th December the Japs were right across the island. The dockyard got more and more shelling and our troops were gradually pushed back. The Japs put up a battery at North Point and so now in the dockyard we were under a crossfire from Kowloon and North Point. This went on until 25th December. During daylight hours

we were continually putting fires out, building or repairing sand bag posts etc., getting our food where we could. At night I slept in different parts of the yard but usually with the police near the Main Gate, being a central position, and used to go round all the posts at different times to see that everything was all right. Commander Craven was in charge of the defences and I helped him. Often, and especially towards the end, we had an alarm during the night and stood to: generally it was a report that a boat was crossing the harbour, and we always stood to just before daybreak and just after sunset. But they never came our way.

The fall of Wong Nei Chong Gap was a critical loss that effectively split the island in two. The Japanese used their artillery and dive bombers almost continuously as their troops pushed against the defence positions on Mount Nicholson and The Ridge to its south. Naval, Royal Army Ordinance Corps and Royal Army Service Corps personnel defended and counter-attacked until The Ridge finally fell on the 21st. A few survivors escaped to join those who were attempting to defend Repulse Bay and protect the civilians there.

As battle raged during 22nd-24th, brave pockets of resistance at Mount Cameron, Leighton Hill, Wanchai Gap, Middle Gap and all around Victoria

were holding up the Japanese advance. Repulse Bay fell on 22nd December and the defenders were ordered back to reinforce Stanley. Many of them were killed, or captured and later executed at Eucliffe, a large castle on the north shore of Repulse Bay. One of the groups, led by Major Young of the Royal Rifles, managed to escape by boat. Having made their way to Round Island, they hid onboard the grounded and abandoned HMS *Thracian*, remaining there until forced to surrender two days later.

On Christmas Day 1941, after 17 days of hard fighting, Sir Mark Young, Governor of Hong Kong, and General Maltby GOC Hong Kong, offered an unconditional surrender to the Japanese forces. The total Hong Kong forces casualties were approximately 4,414 killed, wounded and missing. Naval forces had suffered 148 casualties, 119 of which were either killed or missing. Crowther's account closes the chapter:

. . . in the morning of the 26th the Japanese Army marched into the dockyard and took all our arms . . . The Japs informed us we were their prisoners and would have to obey their orders. We were then moved from one part of the dockyard to another. The Japs apparently had no clear idea what they wanted to do with us, but eventually made up their minds that they did not want us

in the dockyard. We were then ordered to the China Fleet Club, a few hundred yards down the street. When we got there, carrying all our luggage, other Japs, apparently very angry, ordered us back to the Yard. So we went back rather exhausted and slept where we could in the Yard that night. They made no attempt to feed us . . . but we got along as there was food about in dumps, but water was the chief difficulty as the fighting had destroyed the main water supply.

On the 28th we were bundled out of the Yard carrying all our luggage and sent to Murray Barracks, where most of our Army was. Our Army officers informed us that there was no room for us, but that did not affect the Japs and eventually we squeezed in somehow after a good deal of trouble. On the 30th at 0700 hours we were fallen in and marched down after several hours' waiting to the ferry. We were then all packed in like sardines into a ferry which was grossly overloaded and taken across the harbour and landed at Kowloon, some three miles from where we were going to, instead of at a pier quite close to our new camp. We were then marched a long way round, up and down crowded streets, carrying all we had, in order presumably to show us to the local Chinese. The Chinese, however, did not look at all happy and simply looked at us in a dazed silence. The whole road was littered with gear people could no longer carry. I carried a camp bed, blankets, mess utensils, boots and

shoes, and as many towels, socks, shorts, vests and uniform suits etc. I could cram in – enough to last me one year. Little did I think what I carried would have to last me three years eight months with practically no replacements: in fact, most of what I am wearing now (4th October 1945) is what I carried then. I continually dropped my heavy packages and sat in the road until a Jap came along with a fixed bayonet and kicked me up. Eventually I got a Chinese coolie from the large numbers at the side of the road to carry part of my luggage and then a great number of others did the same, and thus I arrived at Shamshuipo Camp at about 1700 with all my gear including the bed that I started off with, completely dead beat. The Japs never gave us any food or water all that day, but we got water and a half a cup of rice that night, but we were too tired to do anything. The camp was in a filthy mess, about a foot of dirt and rubble everywhere, no beds or furniture, no windows, and very few doors to the huts. I was one of the few who had a bed, the others just lay down on the dirt for the night.

Now we started our prisoner of war life.

Mrs MS Davis' letter to her son, Lieutenant Walter Davis RNR, who was interned at Camp N, near Argyle Street in Kowloon. [Colin Aitchison]

The Japanese post-mark can be seen on the right of the envelope. [Colin Aitchison]

7.5.44

FROM: MRS. M.S. DAVIS
18 GLOUCESTER. ROAD
BISHOPSTON. BRISTOL.

DEAR WALTER
GLAD TO HEAR FROM YOU. ALL ARE WELL. HOPE TO SEE YOU SOON
LOVE
MOTHER

Censorship does not allow great prose... [Colin Aitchison]

OPERATION LION AUGUST 1945

It was just over a century since Britain had taken Hong Kong and it was now lost. Almost overnight most of that century's achievement disappeared. The rule of law, amenities such as water, gas, electricity and food supplies; commercial endeavour, trade and businesses floundered. The remnants of British military resistance were rounded up and marched off to barbaric prison camps at Kowloon and Sham Shui Po. All British citizens – men, women and children – were interned at Stanley Camp, where the existing prison was located.

Conditions were harsh and primitive in the extreme; the death rate was high. Some military prisoners were transferred to equally barbaric camps in Japan, and some were drowned *en route* as the ship carrying them was torpedoed by an American submarine.

Captain John Wells, then serving in *HMS Swiftsure*, remembers hearing on 15th August 1945 the voice of British Prime Minister Clement Atlee, broadcast from every loudspeaker in Sydney, announce the end of the war. At 1400 the same day *Swiftsure* set sail for Hong Kong via Manus and Subic Bay. Their orders were to proceed to Hong Kong to take the surrender of the Japanese and to rescue prisoners-of-war and internees.

Commander Craven, the senior naval POW, and a Japanese envoy were flown out from Hong Kong to *HMS Indomitable* to settle the terms of entry. On 30th August Admiral Harcourt and his staff transferred to *Swiftsure* and the Allied fleet steamed into Victoria harbour. The liberation of Hong Kong, known as Operation Lion, had begun.

On 29th August, the British Government issued the following communiqué to the people of Hong Kong:

Rear Admiral Harcourt is lying outside Hong Kong with a very strong fleet. The Naval dockyard is to be ready for his arrival by noon today. Admiral Harcourt will enter the harbour having transferred his flag to the cruiser Swiftsure *which will be accompanied by destroyers and submarines. The capital ships will follow as soon as a passage has been swept. The fleet includes two aircraft carriers, the* Indomitable *and the* Venerable, *the battleship* Anson *and the cruiser* Euryalus.

Commander MacRitchie, on board the Canadian anti-aircraft carrier, *HMCS Prince Robert*, recorded:

On both sides all the way up the channel we could see the havoc wrought by British and American planes in earlier

The cruiser HMS Swiftsure, with Admiral Harcourt embarked, enters Hong Kong via Lei Mun Gap on 30th August 1945. [Colin Aitchison]

Once the harbour was cleared of mines, the capital ships followed. HMS Indomitable, flagship of the fleet, entered a harbour littered with wrecks. [FormAsia Books Ltd]

months. It would appear that Japanese policy had been not to repair the demolition damage created by the British prior to the fall of Hong Kong, or by the allied planes. With the exception of two old crocks the harbour was destitute of Japanese fighting ships. We proceeded to the Kowloon side while Swiftsure set about dropping anchor close in to Hong Kong dockyard. A Canadian ship would be the first allied warship to go alongside a jetty in the colony since war [had] begun.

Small groups of Chinese, intermingled with whites, watched from without the dock gates as we eased our way in. At the dockyard gate was a Japanese sentry. There was no frantic waving or demonstrations until three platoons of Prince Robert's men, in full marching order, complete with fixed bayonets, clashed over the gangplank at the captain's order, 'Secure'. It was then that the crowd broke loose, left the Japanese staring blankly, and surged on to the wharves.

It took our men only a matter of minutes to accomplish the occupation of the Kowloon dockyard area. [There were about 1,500 Japanese soldiers in Kowloon dockyard.] Across the harbour in Hong Kong the Royal Navy units were enjoying equal success. The Japanese soldiers were speedily rounded up and moved outside the gates to their military quarters across the street. There were no untoward incidents.

HMS Indomitable *enters Victoria Harbour with her aircraft ranged on deck. [Captain RJ McGarel-Groves RM]*

The first men to land at the Hong Kong dockyard were sailors and marines from *HMS Swiftsure* led by Commander WLM Brown DSC. They were met by a Japanese officer who asked, 'Would you mind waiting for the Chief of Staff ?' to which Commander Brown famously replied, 'We have no further need of the Japanese Chief of Staff. My orders are to clear the dockyard of all Japanese.'

The 500 men from *Swiftsure* and *Euryalus* cleared the dockyard by that evening. The White Ensign

A view from the deck of HMS Venerable [Captain RJ McGarel-Groves RM]

was raised to the sound of a bugle, with a Royal Marine Guard of Honour.

The immediate tasks were to secure the streets, disperse looters, round up the remaining Japanese forces and assist the Allied POWs and civilians who were in obvious need of help after some three and a half years of hardship. Royal Marines from *HMS Anson* liberated the POWs from Sham Shui Po camp, including Colonel Giles and his surviving RM Detachment.

Ships' personnel were divided into two groups: Brown Force (led by Commander Brown) and Kennedy Force (led by Commander AR Kennedy). Men for these two parties were drawn from the *Anson, Swiftsure, Euryalus* and *Indomitable*. Brown Force took over Aberdeen, Taikoo, Stanley and the Peak, whilst Kennedy Force patrolled Victoria. The two forces comprised about 550 men each; 450 were on active patrol, and the remainder handled administrative, medical and transport duties.

Warships have no room for blank charges in wartime, and so one of the first jobs was to scour the ammunition dumps the Japanese had left all over the island (many of which had been captured from the British in 1941), looking for blanks with which to fire the twenty-one gun salute when the surrender was signed. Admiral Harcourt drove to the Stanley

Japanese kamikaze boat coxswains on Lamma raise their arms in surrender to the Navy. [JSPRS] *

Internment Camp for the flag-raising ceremony. A Royal Marine escort noted that the internees were 'walking skeletons'. Captain John Wells was also there: 'It was amazing to see their reactions to fresh bread, English cigarettes and chocolate. Some of us sampled their daily bread made of rice and linseed oil. It tasted like sawdust, but they thought it a great delicacy.'

The echoes of this moving occasion remain in

Japanese taken in the dockyard line up to be searched by a marine while a guard stands at the ready. [JSPRS]

---

* *[JSPRS]* is an abbreviation for *Joint Services Public Relations Service*

the last words of the Admiral's speech to the 2,000 ex-internees: ' . . . I only want to say one thing. The motive that has inspired all my men, all the blue jackets, to get here as quickly as possible – which we have done – has been, really . . . you people.'

As the Japanese had technically surrendered on 14th August, many of the civil service internees had already left the camps and made their way back to government buildings. The pre-war Colonial Secretary, Mr FC Gimson, left the Stanley camp and was directed by the British Government on 17th August to restore British sovereignty and administration until the arrival of Admiral Harcourt. As R Hutcheon writes in his book, SCMP: The First Eighty Years:

> Hong Kong people crawled out of the ruins of Japanese occupation dazed, demoralised and destitute, to return to a city that had ground to a halt under alien administration. The population had dwindled to about 600,000. . . and there was hardly a heartbeat left in the city. Yet, as the internees struggled out of Stanley and the flag went up. . . the most obvious thing to do was to set up house again and go back to work. And so within hours of the gates of Stanley being opened, the first small signs of new life appeared. The trams were running on 20 August, followed soon by the ferries. And from then on it never looked back.

Royal Marines from the battleship HMS Anson *round up some Japanese officers for questioning. The Japanese officer with arms folded, in the centre, is Lieutenant Colonel Kanazawa, head of the Gendarmerie, Kowloon. [JSPRS]*

The primary aim was to resume living and working practices in the colony. Years of ill treatment and malnutrition had taken their toll and whilst the civil servants and those responsible for public utilities quickly addressed their tasks, they were really only capable of light duties.

One of the major problems of the period following the liberation was that much of the population had been decimated during the war years, creating a shortage of manpower. Civilian organisations therefore drew on naval personnel to make up their depleted numbers. Naval doctors worked at Stanley while the Harbour Office, with Commander Jolly at its head, was reactivated. The task of policing the colony also fell to the Navy, as the police force was not strong enough to act independently. They too were physically in very poor shape. Three years in an internment camp had left them in such a weakened state that at first they were only fit to work as interpreters for the patrols.

A proclamation on 1st September established a military administration. The next day Admiral Harcourt was appointed Commander-in-Chief and Head of the Military Administration (in essence, the Governor), and Gimson temporarily assumed the role of Lieutenant Governor.

At Kai Tak airfield, Mobile Operation Naval Air Base No. 8 (MONAB) was set up. These bases were established on captured and liberated islands in the latter years of the war to provide sites for squadrons to rest and to repair aircraft away from the cramped conditions onboard aircraft carriers. The Royal Air Force was also based at Kai Tak, on the far side of the airfield.

The MONAB unit found daily work for about 2,000 of the Japanese prisoners of war housed at Sham Shui Po, previously occupied by Allied troops. Many of them were employed in cleaning aircraft, digging, and general tasks, and were still there at Christmas 1945.

On 12th September, 13 days after Harcourt's arrival, 3 Commando Brigade (comprising Brigade HQ, 1 & 5 Army Commandos, 42 & 44 Royal Marine Commandos and Royal Marine Signals and Engineer units) arrived in Hong Kong. Brigadier CR Harding DSO RM and his men were initially given responsibility for patrolling and policing the New Territories against the considerable looting and rioting that was taking place there.

Eventually, commando forces took over the tasks carried out by the Brown and Kennedy forces. Admiral Harcourt later paid special tribute to the important role that the Commandos played in

Captain R J McGarel-Groves, Officer Commanding the RM detachment of HMS Venerable, *checks surrendered Japanese weapons at Whitfield Camp, Kowloon, where the Japanese troops were interned. [JSPRS]*

Admiral Sir Bruce Fraser, Commander-in-Chief of the British Pacific Fleet, Chinese observer Major General Pan Hwa Kue and Rear Admiral Harcourt at the surrender ceremony. [JSPRS]

Captain Eccles points out a clause in the British terms for the surrender of arms by the Japanese. [JSPRS]

The Japanese naval representative, Vice Admiral Ruitako Fujita, signs the surrender document. [JSPRS]

INSTRUMENT OF SURRENDER

We, Major General Umekichi Okada and Vice Admiral Ruitaro Fujita, in virtue of the unconditional surrender to the Allied Powers of all Japanese Armed Forces and all forces under Japanese control wherever situated, as proclaimed in Article Two of the Instrument of Surrender signed in Tokio Bay on 2nd September, 1945, on behalf of the Emperor of Japan and the Japanese Imperial Headquarters, do hereby unconditionally surrender ourselves and all forces under our control to Rear Admiral Cecil Halliday Jepson Harcourt, C.B., C.B.E., and undertake to carry out all such instructions as may be given by him or under his authority, and to issue all necessary orders for the purpose of giving effect to all his instructions.

Given under our hands this 16th day of September, 1945, at Government House, Hong Kong.

In the presence of

On behalf of the Government of the United Kingdom.

On behalf of the Commander-in-Chief, China Theatre.

海軍中將

藤田類太郎

陸軍少將

岡田梅吉

The instrument of surrender signed by Major General Okada and Vice Admiral Fujita, witnessed by Rear Admiral Harcourt. [Captain RJ McGarel-Groves RM (Retd.)]

rebuilding Hong Kong: 'They had greatly enhanced the reputation of the British Services in the Far East both by their smart appearance and by their good sense of humour.'

If humour had been in short supply during the occupation, the liberating forces brought a more than ample supply with them. Captain Wells recorded:

Some of the officers, impatient with the continual delays in the signing of the surrender, decided to hold it themselves. A Japanese General, in the form of a torpedo officer, was captured, the captain was hurriedly promoted to the rank of Governor-General, and in front of an admiring audience and representatives of the press (who thought they were coming to the real thing), and accompanied by a fourteen-gun salute, the Japanese envoy signed a complete, unconditional surrender – without trousers!

On 16th September, the official instrument of surrender was signed by the Japanese at Government House under the supervision of Admiral Harcourt. The last act of the *Swiftsure* landing parties was to line the route near the Queen's Pier through which admirals, generals and Japanese passed on their way to and from Government House. Royal Marines from *HMS Anson* provided the Guard of Honour.

On re-occupied Hong Kong Island, a Chinese woman re-commencing work is paid in rice. [JSPRS]

The Services also brought a welcome return to normality on the social scene. A children's party was held on board *HMS Swiftsure*, at which Captain Wells observed:

The Chaplain arrived from the Stanley camp accompanied by all the children in the 9-11 age group, who, after looking around the ship – during which no one fell off the mast or wrecked too many valuable fittings – they settled down to tea in the wardroom. Never has so much been eaten by so many in so short a time. Before taking them to see a cinema show consisting of two

'Mickey Mouses', the First Lieutenant, as senior father on board, carried out the duties of 'Uncle Potty' in a most efficient manner. One small boy was sick on the padre on the way home – and he had foolishly eaten the whole of his chocolate ration!

On 10th September, the *South China Morning Post* observed, 'A sure sign of Hong Kong's gradual return to normal conditions was the sight of an energetic number of white figures running about on the Cricket Club's ground yesterday, when two naval

On Kai Tak Airstrip, ratings from HMS Indomitable *re-establish communications circuits.*
[JSPRS]

Naval officers on the first train to leave Kowloon. Lieutenant P Morris and Sub-Lieutenant R Spurway from HMS Indomitable (pictured onboard) were responsible for the initial re-organisation of the railway. [JSPRS]

Mr RC Dinnie (in shorts on the right) the Dockyard cashier interned at the fall of Hong Kong, with RM guards supervising the issue of rice to labourers employed in the clearing and reconstruction of the dockyard. [JSPRS]

Sub-Lieutenant RC Martin, in charge of a naval party from HMS Venerable, 'liberated' 90 horses and formed a mounted naval patrol. The picture shows them on patrol in Kowloon City. [JSPRS]

Displaying samurai swords, trophies of their occupation of Kai Tak Airstrip, are men from HMS Indomitable. On horseback are Commander T Jameson, Captain DC Mahoney RM, and Lieutenant Commander BAC Nation. [JSPRS]

Mr FC Gimson, the British Colonial Secretary (In trilby and black shorts) meets Rear Admiral Harcourt with Commander Donald Craven, the Senior Naval POW. [JSPRS]

Five veterans rest after the Fleet Veterans Parade on 22nd August 1995. Back: Buck Buckle (Swiftsure), Cyril Dixon (Illustrious), Bill Rumsey (Implacable); front: Arthur Wickes (Indefatigable), Bas White (Indomitable). [JSPRS]

Admiral Harcourt reviews the Royal Marines at Government House. [Public Records Office]

The hospital ship Oxfordshire at Kowloon docks to embark Japanese prisoners of war. [Public Records Office]

A group of WRNS in 1945. [Susan Wells]

Ex-internees provided the motive for Admiral Harcourt to relieve Hong Kong 'as quickly as possible'. [Kathleen Harland]

The climax of this new-found light-heartedness was Victory Day, on 9th October, when '. . . bright sunshine, happy crowds, brilliant uniforms, martial music and flags formed the background to the official celebrations.' The march past the Hongkong and Shanghai Bank took approximately fifteen minutes. The military administration in Hong Kong continued for eight months, until Sir Mark Young, who had been imprisoned by the Japanese in both Wusong and Taiwan, returned to his post as Governor on 1st May 1946.

It is difficult so many years on to capture the feelings of those for whom this ordeal had just ended, but a letter published not long after the arrival of the Fleet expressed the feelings of at least one member of the public:

Polite, neat, kind and forebearing, the members of the Relief Staff are carrying out their duty to the satisfaction of all people. We see more sympathy with the poor in the streets than show of pride in being a victorious force. The Admiral, Commanders and Seamen all alike put on smiling faces wherever they be met with. Despite having fought for years, as some officers of the Swiftsure said to me, their calm behaviour and quiet personality still exist. This is a credit of the British Navy.

teams were engaged in a normal match.' Only the scoreboard was missing, having, like so much of Hong Kong's woodwork and furniture, been used for firewood during the occupation. Evening entertainment too, underwent something of a renaissance. The *South China Morning Post* reported on a dance in Stanley:

Great enthusiasm was shown by the ex-internees over two dances, the Hokey-Kokey and the Conga. These dances are very popular in Great Britain and America, but naturally, new to Stanley folks. Several of the Stanley ladies are developing into first class Jitterbugs under the expert tuition of the young rhythm-minded members of the fleet.

THE ROYAL NAVY AND THE ROYAL HONG KONG YACHT CLUB

An interesting footnote to the huge part the Royal Navy played in setting Hong Kong back on its feet after the Japanese occupation, is the re-building of the Yacht Club. The Navy had always played a major part in yachting in the colony. Indeed, in the early years the Navy *was* yachting. The first regatta, in February 1845, was organised by the Navy, and so it remained until the Yacht Club came into existence at the end of 1869. From then until 1941 yachting thrived. The Yacht Club became the Royal Hong Kong Yacht Club in 1894, and in 1940 a prestigious new clubhouse was opened on the site of the old naval magazines on Kellett Island. Shortly after it was opened, the Japanese invaded, and for the next four years the club's members became more used to the sparse internment camp than to the luxurious new surroundings they had built for themselves.

By the time British administration was re-established in Hong Kong, the new clubhouse was a wreck, and although the officers and men of *HMS Vengance* officially reopened it in September 1945, much work remained. As the men of *HMS Vengeance*

set-to with a will, all three services used the club for recreation, sailing the Royal Naval Sailing Association's 14-foot dinghies carried by the ships of the British Pacific Fleet. When *Vengeance* sailed for home, she donated her dinghies to the club and restoration work was continued by *HMS Adamant*, the submarine depot ship, starting, of course, with the re-construction of the main bar!

As in the early days of the colony, for the first few years after the war yachting and the Royal Navy were synonymous, and the Service ran Kellett Island on behalf of the yachting community. By December 1946 the Royal Hong Kong Yacht Club was ready to resume control of its affairs, and at an Extraordinary General Meeting on the 12th, the Commodore of the club, Noel Croucher, espoused the club's gratitude for all the Royal Navy's hard work and generosity.

On 17th September 1995, during the 50th anniversary of the liberation celebrations, a commemorative party was held at the Royal Hong Kong Yacht Club. Organised by a committee chaired by Commodore Melson, a display of modern military capability was displayed off Kellett Island by the sailors and marines of *HMS Plover* and the Wessex helicopters of the RAF's 28 (AC) Squadron. An Army band beat retreat and a lone Gurkha piper

played as the flag was lowered for the sunset ceremony. It was a poignant reminder of the significance of the liberation of Hong Kong and the enduring relationship between the Royal Navy and the Royal Hong Kong Yacht Club. ■

The Royal Hong Kong Yacht Club as it stands today. [JSPRS]

Commodore Melson and Lieutenant Nick Doyle, the Gunnery Officer of HMS Tamar, *represent the Senior Service at the last Remembrance Day Parade under British rule, November 1996. [JSPRS]*

COMMUNIST CONUNDRUMS

POST-WAR YEARS

For the first few years after the Japanese surrender, the Commander-in-Chief British Pacific Fleet flew his flag ashore in Hong Kong. In October 1948, however, he moved to Singapore with a new title of Commander-in-Chief Far East Station. This move implemented plans laid in 1934, but delayed by the war, to establish Singapore as a major world dockyard and base. Hong Kong was re-designated an Operational and Training Base under the command of a Commodore, and the major fleet units left for Singapore.

Among the defensive measures initiated on the approach of the Chinese Communist Army in the late 1940s was the re-creation of the Hong Kong Flotilla. This unusually motley throng consisted of 10 Seaward Defence Motor Launches (SDML), reclassified from Harbour Defence Motor Launches; four WWII Motor Minesweepers (MMS); Admiralty

HMS Belfast, *Flagship of the Pacific Fleet, 1946. [Public Records Office]*

Motor Fishing Vessels (MFV) equipped as Inshore Minesweepers; and eight Landing Craft Assault vessels (LCA) with one crew to each two craft, one of the pair being gun- armed, and the other equipped with a flame thrower – an effective weapon against sturdily built wooden junks.

Another measure saw *3 Commando Brigade Royal Marines*, having played a major role in rebuilding Hong Kong during 1945-47, returning to the colony in 1949. It was to be a short stay, however, as events

in 1950 saw the Brigade re-deployed for active service in Malaya.

As the Communist threat subsided, craft were put into reserve or disposed of, with the exception of the SDMLs, which retained the title of Hong Kong Flotilla. They were employed on standing patrols in the Pearl River estuary to deter communist intrusions and to support the embargo on exporting strategic goods to China.

Although units of the 5th Cruiser Squadron, the

8th Destroyer Flotilla, the 1st Escort Flotilla and the 3rd and 4th Frigate Flotillas (or Frigate Squadrons, as they were known after 1952) continued to call in for Docking and Essential Defects, or leave and recreation, there was no longer the concentration of force seen in pre-war times.

For a period in the 1950s, the 3rd and 4th Frigate Flotillas were each commanded by a captain and consisted of four ships. The former was made up of HM Ships Crane (the flotilla leader), Modeste, Amethyst and Opossum, while the latter's ships were Bay Class Frigates, including St Brides Bay and Cardigan Bay. The leader of the flotilla was easily recognisable by a large black band around the top of the funnel and the absence of pennant numbers on the ship's side.

THE AMETHYST INCIDENT

HMS Amethyst is perhaps the best known of these ships, as it was caught in the crossfire of the Nationalist and Communist Chinese forces in 1949. She was going up to Nanking in April 1949 to relieve HMS Consort as guard ship at the British Embassy,

HMS Amethyst *en route to Hong Kong from Shanghai after her sprint down the Yangtse, 1949. [JSPRS]*

and was to stand by there in case fighting made it necessary to evacuate British and Commonwealth nationals. To ensure there would be no mistake about her nationality, a large Union Jack was painted on both her sides. In spite of this precaution, she came under heavy shelling from Communist batteries along the north bank of the Yangtse, running her aground and killing 17 British sailors – including the medical officer – and seriously wounding 10 more, among whom was her commanding officer, Lieutenant-Commander Skinner. He and another sailor later died of their wounds.

Attempts by the 10,000-ton cruiser HMS London and the frigate HMS Black Swan to reach the stricken ship were thwarted by more heavy shelling and further casualties. Fortunately, the Amethyst managed to refloat herself and travel a few miles up river to the Ta Sha South Channel. Here she lay, repairing as far as possible, and embarking medical supplies and assistance. For several months she remained at her anchorage whilst negotiations with the People's Liberation Army (PLA) were conducted in an attempt to ensure a safe conduct down river to Shanghai. Eventually it became apparent that the Communists had little or no intention of granting safe conduct for the Amethyst, and instead were determined to keep her in the Yangtse for their own purposes.

Conditions onboard worsened. Fuel and food supplies dwindled and the crew, already suffering severely from ravaging mosquitoes and rats, were placed on half rations. After waiting three months, Lieutenant-Commander Kerans decided to make for the river mouth. There was no pilot onboard, and in the pitch darkness it would have been almost impossible to see the shore marks. At 2220 on 30th July, Kerans gave the order to slip, and the *Amethyst* began the 140-mile dash to safety. Once again she

Simon DM, the Amethyst's *cat.* [JSPRS]

A bird's eye view of the northern part of Hong Kong Island and Tsim Sha Tsui taken from Mid-levels c1940s. [HK Museum of History]

83

suffered heavy fire from Communist shore batteries, and for the next eight hours the entire ship's company were at either action or at damage stations.

The perilous journey was widely reported and earned signals of congratulation and tributes to the skill and determination of the *Amethyst*'s crew from all over the world. Lieutenant-Commander Kerans received the Distinguished Service Order, and Telegraphist Jack French, who remained on continuous wireless watch for six days and nights, was awarded the Distinguished Service Medal.

Simon, the ship's cat, also earned a decoration. He had been injured during the shelling and had nevertheless played his part by keeping down the rats that threatened the ship's rapidly dwindling food supplies. He became the first cat to receive the Dickin Medal, regarded as the animals' VC.

HMS Ceylon *decommissions, 1959. [Tim Reeder]*

A DANGEROUS PATROL

On 3rd September 1953, *HMML 1323* was attacked by Chinese patrol craft. Usually these patrols passed with a wave of greeting but on this occassion the Chinese opened fire forcing all personnel to take cover in the lightly armoured bridge. The crew did not return fire and as they tried tried to manouevre out of range, a four-inch shell hit the bridge, killing two and mortally wounding the commanding officer, a young Lieutenant. With a cool head the Leading Stoker kept one engine going at excess speed, and went on deck to engage the second steering position at the stern. With the help of survivors, the launch made it back to the jetty at Tai O.

THE FAR EAST FLEET

A typical programme for ships in those days is unclear, but it seems that the summer months were spent to the north, often in Japanese waters. Shore visits were frequent, and a hike up Mount Fuji seems to have been a 'must' on many a sailor's visit to the

Royal Naval Dockyard, 1950s. [HK Museum of History]

Land of the Rising Sun. Visits were common as well to Singapore, and to the annual South East Asian Treaty Organisation (SEATO) exercise, which involved many Allied navies. At Hong Kong, three-month refits would be followed by work-ups and trials in the Mirs Bay and Tolo Harbour region. During refits the Fleet Accommodation Base on the left-hand side of the main entrance to the dockyard provided dormitory-type quarters for about 60 personnel. The new, shore-based *HMS Tamar* was also used, and when necessary, the China Fleet Club.

Post-war austerity bit hard. Hong Kong did not have a guard ship, so the Emergency Destroyer routine was employed instead. All ships in the area were classified Hong Kong Defence Force, and came under the operational control of Commodore Hong Kong. To conserve fuel, all warships would, if alongside a jetty, shut down the boilers. One ship, a frigate or a destroyer, would be always at immediate notice for sea and would normally moor to a buoy in midstream for speedy action in case of an emergency. After a 24-hour spell of duty she would return alongside and her relief would go out to the buoy.

While *HMS St Bride's Bay* was Emergency Destroyer, an incident occurred involving one of the regular ferries from Hong Kong to Macau. The ferry

The post-war HMS Tamar was originally located in Wellington Barracks, adjacent to the dockyard. [Tim Reeder]

had just cleared the harbour entrance when it was intercepted by Communist gunboats, which signalled their intention to send a boarding party. They were apparently in pursuit of a Nationalist Chinese general travelling on the ferry. The ferry warned Hong Kong by radio, and *St Bride's Bay* steamed out at full speed, firing four-inch shells directly ahead of the gunboats, which then made off. From accounts of those who served in the East at this time, such an incident was not unique.

The Korean War led to a huge build-up of forces in Hong Kong as the colony became a staging post for ships, troops and aircraft en route to the war zone. From September 1950 to July 1953, Hong Kong was the forward support base for the carriers, cruisers, frigates and destroyers that were always on station off the west coast of Korea. During both the Korean conflict and the 1956 Suez crisis, ships were diverted to respond to the changing political situation, in particular HM *Ships Unicorn* and *Crane*.

HMS Unicorn paid more visits to Hong Kong than perhaps any other warship in the Far East during the Korean War. She was a huge Aircraft Repair Vessel, on the 'tramlines' run – Singapore, Hong Kong, Iwakuni, Sasebo and Kure – then back to Singapore for another cargo of stores. On one voyage, while transporting about 10 Canberras to Iwakuni for the RAF, she received a distress call from a British merchant ship that was being attacked by a Chinese Nationalist destroyer in the vicinity of Round Island. Once on the scene, however, the very appearance of the *HMS Unicorn*, which looked similar to an aircraft carrier ready to launch its planes, was enough to encourage the Chinese to beat a hasty retreat.

Another ship that visited Hong Kong in the 1950s was the old aircraft carrier *HMS Venerable*,

Filling in the dry dock. The Navy paid a contractor to carry out the work – he simply erected a collection booth by the dock and charged construction vehicles that were only too happy to have such a convenient spoil dump in Central. [Tim Reeder]

which had been with the fleet when it returned to Hong Kong in August 1945, at the end of the war. When the British Government sold it to the Netherlands later in the 1950s, she was renamed *Karel Doorman*. The Dutch Navy eventually sold her to Argentina, where she achieved notoriety as the Argentinian flagship *25 de Mayo* during the Falklands conflict in 1982.

THE CLOSURE OF THE DOCKYARD 1957-1959

In 1957, the Navy employed approximately 4,500 workmen of varying skill levels in the dockyard. A further 250 or so Europeans held managerial positions and about 250 people performed clerical

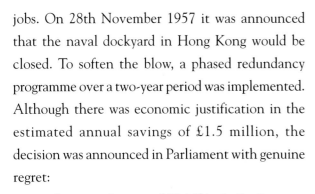

The Fleet Regatta of 1958, held in Junk Bay.
A crew waiting for the start.

A motor launch of the Hong Kong Flotilla.

HMS Newfoundland *at the finish line. [Tim Reeder]*

jobs. On 28th November 1957 it was announced that the naval dockyard in Hong Kong would be closed. To soften the blow, a phased redundancy programme over a two-year period was implemented. Although there was economic justification in the estimated annual savings of £1.5 million, the decision was announced in Parliament with genuine regret:

> . . . *future requirements of HM Ships in Far Eastern waters will no longer justify the maintenance of a full scale refitting dockyard in Hong Kong . . . The long*

association of the dockyard with Hong Kong [55 years from the foundation ceremony] and the loss of employment for many workers which must inevitably result from the closure, are factors which have weighed heavily with Her Majesty's Ministers.

Concerns over the decision brought little formal protest due to the excellent liaison between the Navy and the Hong Kong Government regarding resettlement, and early reassurances that everything possible would be done to protect the livelihood of

those affected. The redundancies commenced in January 1958, with an anticipated rate of discharge of around 130 men a month. It was hoped that some would find work before dismissal, whilst others would need the help of the newly formed Employment Liaison Office. The Commodore invited prospective employers to visit the dockyard to learn about the skills of the workforce.

All went well until the beginning of March 1958, when workers staged a squat-down protest against the dismissals. It ended peacefully a few hours later, however, and there were no repetitions, due probably to the strenuous efforts of both Service and civil authorities to help find new jobs. By 28th November 1959, all 4,650 redundancies were completed. About one-sixth of the men were without new employment.

For the Hong Kong Government, one positive aspect of the closure of the dockyard was that new roads could be built from Central to Wanchai. Most of the released land had been naval, but the section to the east, next to the Police Headquarters, was Army land the Navy had used for administrative and living accommodations which were lost when *HMS Tamar* was scuttled. In 1959 the Hong Kong Government paid the War Department HK$24 million for this area, but it was not handed over until 1962. Harcourt Road, a new street linking Connaught Road with Gloucester Road, was named in honour of Admiral Harcourt.

Although it was always intended that the Navy retain 'a small maintenance and operation base', the decision to retain a sizeable portion of its old waterfront and create a naval base in Central was not made until August 1959. The remainder was handed over to the Hong Kong Government on 28th November 1959. On the same day, the Commodore in Charge received a farewell message from the Civil Lords of the Admiralty:

HMY Britannia *paid its first visit to the colony in 1959. Here, the Duke of Edinburgh is greeted as he arrives at Queen's Pier. With him is the Governor, Sir Robert Black. [Tim Reeder]*

The closing of Hong Kong dockyard ends a long chapter of honourable service to the Royal Navy in Hong Kong for well over half a century. In that time, generations of dockyard workers created and upheld a great tradition of quick work, versatile skill and devoted loyalty. Their reputation for these qualities was known and praised around the world. Their Lordships desire to express their gratitude for all the benefits thus bestowed upon the Royal Navy. Their deep regret that the Yard had to be closed is mingled with pride in the historic achievements of its workers.

The Commodore's car, with driver Lai Chung. [Tim Reeder]

SWINGING INTO THE SIXTIES

The new *HMS Tamar*, which replaced the dockyard, was originally in Wellington Barracks. The Army had transferred it to the Navy in 1946. This site backed onto the waterfront and was adjacent to the dockyard on its eastern boundary. Until 1959 the dockyard and this administrative base existed side by side, but independently.

Following the release of the naval area, a new site gradually emerged between 1959 and 1962 in the form of a compact, modern naval base between Harcourt Road and the waterfront. Old naval buildings were pulled down, and some were used to help fill in the dry dock; by 1962 the new accommodations and quarters, having moved several hundred yards from the eastern end, were ready in the western end of the old dockyard. The primary task of this new base was to provide facilities for the minesweepers based in Hong Kong, and for one frigate or destroyer carrying out self-maintenance.

In the late 1950s, operations in Borneo against the Communist insurgents in Malaysia required Hong Kong-based reinforcements. In October 1958 the 120th Minesweeping Squadron, consisting of

HMS Glentham *of the 120th Minesweeping Squadron passing visiting American warships.* [FOSF]

HM *Ships Damerham, Darsham, Davenham, Glentham* and *Hovingham* arrived and were placed under the control of the Commodore Hong Kong. These ships were backed up in October 1962 by the 8th Minesweeping Squadron of *Dufton, Penston* and *Lanton*. With Hong Kong as the base, these

minesweepers carried out numerous Borneo patrols until the confrontation in Malaya ended in 1966. The following year, as part of the United Kingdom's defence economy measures, the ships were transferred to the Inshore Flotilla at Singapore. The plan was that Hong Kong would be supplied when

HMS Eagle, *1965. [FOSF]*

HMS Victorious, *1961. [Fleet Air Arm Museum]*

HMS Albion, *1964. [Fleet Air Arm Museum]*

HMS Albion, *in February 1968. Chinese labourers chip rust and paint
from the flight deck prior to re-painting. [Fleet Air Arm Museum]*

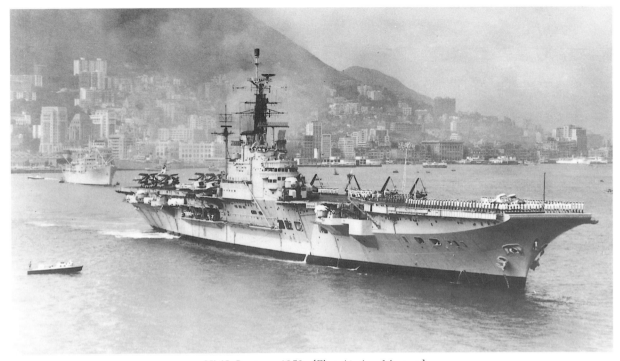

HMS Centaur, 1959. [Fleet Air Arm Museum]

Wasperton, *Wolverton* and *Monkton* completed the Hong Kong Squadron, renamed the 6th Patrol Craft Squadron, after minesweeping equipment was removed from the vessels. The new squadron required a build-up of the necessary technical personnel in the *Tamar* base, and initially the ships' programmes centred on patrols round the colony's many islands, providing assistance, if necessary, to the Marine Police. The force was small, but interestingly enough, it corresponded almost exactly to the force levels during most of the 19th century. Office blocks replaced the receiving ship, the telephone and wireless superceded the dispatch vessel, and the patrol craft was really the gunboat under another name. ◼

necessary with ships from this flotilla and, of course, major warships in the Far East such as *HM Ships Eagle*, *Albion* and *Intrepid* continued to call in with their support frigates and auxiliaries. A guardship, usually a frigate, was stationed in the colony. The last of these was *HMS Chichester*, here from 1974 to March 1976.

In 1969 another policy change occurred. As part of the redeployment of the Far East Fleet, the 6th Mine Countermeasures Squadron, comprising *HM Ships Maxton*, *Boddington*, *Kirkliston*, *Sheraton* and *Hubberston*, was permanently transferred to Hong Kong. The following year they adopted the Chinese dragon as their squadron badge and displayed it on the funnel of each ship. Previously the squadron badge had been a black foot motif derived, by tradition, from the marks stokers left on deck during coaling in the days of steam. In 1971, *Bossington*, *Hubberston* and *Maxton* were replaced by *Beachampton* and *Yarnton*. The following year,

HMS Hampshire, 1969. [FOSF]

HMS Victorious, *in the busy harbour, 1965.* [FOSF]

HMS Lion, *Navy Days, 1963. [Public Records Office]*

Victoria Harbour, 1971. [FOSF]

The Basin in 1973, with Harcourt Road built on former dockyard land. [JSPRS]

HMS Devonshire, *1974. [FOSF]*

HMS Lion, *1963. [FOSF]*

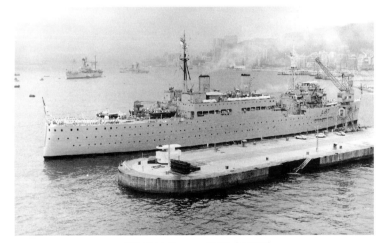

HMS Defiance, *1973. [FOSF]*

HMS Yarmouth, *1974. [FOSF]*

The decommissioning of Bossington, Hubberston *and* Maxton *in 1971. They were replaced by* Beachampton *and* Yarnton, *while the folllowing year the arrival of* Wasperton, Wolverton *and* Monkton *saw the decommissioning of* Kirkleston *and* Sheraton *to form the new look* 'Dragon Squadron'. *[Captain David Whitehead, RN]*

The buoys ashore! [Captain David Whitehead, RN]   HMS Chichester, 1974. [FOSF]

HMS Wolverton, 1982. [JSPRS]

HMS Wolverton *in commission, 1984. [FOSF]*

Later, as the Wolverton Club, *1989. [Trevor Hollingsbee]*

And in 1991, following suspected arson. [Trevor Hollingsbee]

In 1971, the liner Queen Elizabeth, *due to be converted into a floating university in* Victoria Harbour, *caught fire.* HMS Yarnton, *the duty ship, sailed within 10 minutes of being notified and remained on scene for nearly 24 hours, playing a key role in the incident as a command and control vessel. It was all to no avail, and the ship eventually capsized due to the vast quantity of water pumped inboard.*
[Captain David Whitehead RN]

HMS Wasperton, *guardship for the World 505 Sailing Championships in November 1973.*
[Lieutenant Commander RF Bryant RN]

An aerial view of the Basin, 1975. Alongside are visitors RFA Stromness and HMS Blake. [FOSF]

Divisions on the Bull's Nose. Note the foundations for the Prince of Wales Building. [Kathleen Harland]

The Prince of Wales Building as it neared completion in 1978. [FOSF]

HRH Prince Charles onboard HMS Wasperton *during the ceremonies for the opening of the Prince of Wales Building, 1979. [Public Records Office]*

STRENGTH IN SERVICE

THE LOCALLY ENLISTED PERSONNEL DIVISION

Locally Enlisted Personnel (LEP) have served in the ships of the Royal Navy since the 19th century. When the clippers called at Canton before 1842, they engaged mess boys and cooks whilst they were in the Pearl River, and although few Chinese were embarked during the Opium Wars, the fleet quickly settled down in the 1850s to the regular employment of Chinese as cooks and personal servants to the officers. They wore no uniform and were paid from the officers' own pockets.

In 1905 the LEP division was created and formally established as an integral part of the Royal Navy in the Far East. The first LEP division consisted of two Seamen Petty Officers, 50 Able Seamen, seven Stokers and nine Mess Boys. They were employed onboard *HMS Tamar*, the Yangtse River gun boats, armed launches and other craft. LEP wore

The final LEP Divisions, December 1996. [JSPRS]

a uniform consisting of a peaked cap, a serge Chinese-style jacket and badges of rank. Some personal servants were later provided with livery from the slop chest (the ship's source of uniforms).

During the First World War the number of British Regulars in the Garrison and Fleet shrank, and so the number of LEP increased. As the Second World War approached, the numbers of Stokers and Seamen increased again, and by 1939 LEP were employed in every type of ship on the Station. At about the same time the HKRNVR was mobilised; it too included many Chinese.

To prevent information from falling into the hands of the enemy when the Japanese invaded, the main records were destroyed. All LEP (except those away from the colony) were discharged, ordered to destroy all documentary links with the Navy and fade into the civil population. After re-occupation, most of the pre-war LEP reported back for duty. Due to the chaotic state of communications at that time in China and the Far East, it was a lengthy process for many.

Numbers in the Division have continued to fluctuate over the years in response to the political situation. The highest number of LEP serving in the Royal Navy was in 1946, when their ranks boasted over 2,000. It was a busy time in the affairs

Sailors from HMS Tamar salute naval veterans at the Liberation Day Parade, August 1995. [JSPRS]

of Hong Kong as the colony struggled to rebuild a society that had suffered from over three years of hostile Japanese occupation. The LEP were employed in just about every capacity imaginable, from acting as interpreters to levelling disease-ridden residential areas.

In the years that followed, numbers dwindled. The division was down to about 1,000 before increasing again in the 1950s with the outbreak of the Korean War and the conflict with Malaysia. In the 1974 Defence Review, the Ministry of Defence decided to exercise its discretion in the future employment of LEP. Perhaps the saddest part of the decision, which had been made despite the obvious economy of employing LEP fleet-wide, was that for the first time LEP no longer had any

THE UNOFFICIALS

The tradition of Chinese laundrymen, tailors, barbers and shoemakers working onboard Her Majesty's warships dates back to the early 1930s, when they provided a service to ships alongside in Shanghai and in Wei-Hai-Wei. Individual ships' commanding officers would determine the contract terms and conditions for each ship. As they had no official status onboard, they became known as 'the unofficials'.

Gradually, these unofficials began to work onboard when the ships left port. When the fleet relocated from China to Hong Kong and Singapore in 1949, they brought the unofficials with them, and shortly afterwards their administration was taken on by *HMS Tamar*. Instead of individual ships drawing up their own contracts a standard contract was used. From their ranks, a number of unofficials were nominated as contractors, each with the responsibility for a group of ships tasked with providing an onboard laundry service. The contractors, living and working onboard, were in charge of recruiting the laundrymen, and this system remained largely unchanged.

At first they only worked in the Far East, but

The opening of Tamar's *time capsule, January 1997. [JSPRS]*

responsibility other than that of the immediate policing and defence of Hong Kong.

LEP continued to serve with the Navy in Hong Kong, both ashore and at sea. Chinese Senior and Junior Rates flew to Scotland to 'stand by' the five *Peacocks* during build in Aberdeen, before sailing with the ships to Hong Kong. They continued to serve at sea until the final seagoing sailor left *HMS Plover* in September 1996. Naval LEP remain active within Hong Kong. Indeed, the LEP's final duty will be to ferry the last elements of the Garrison to Kai Tak Airport on the evening of 30th June 1997.

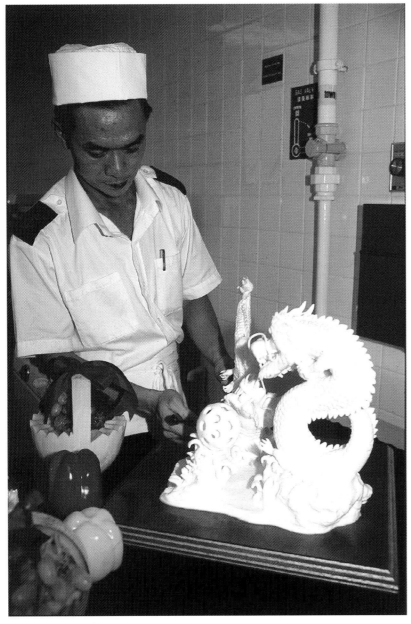

Winning culinary contests …

… and in the galley. [JSPRS]

Maintaining the ship's main armament, the 76mm Oto Melara gun. [JSPRS]

LEP watchkeepers monitor engine instruments in a Peacock's Machinery Control Room. [JSPRS]

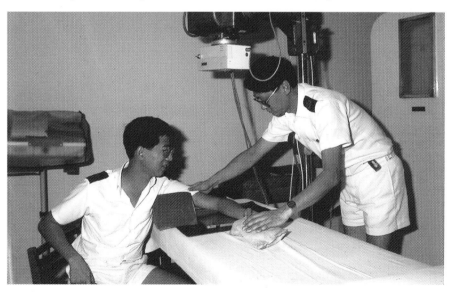

The Sick Bay. [JSPRS]

Members of HMS Tamar's Ships' Company and VIPs, December 1996. [JSPRS]

eventually started sailing with ships returning to the UK after a Far East deployment. They would leave the ship in Aden and return to Hong Kong on the ship coming from the UK as a replacement. This continued until *HMS Belfast* sailed to the UK, via the East coast of America, when the unofficials stayed with the ship until its return to the UK.

Although these men were not subject to naval discipline nor obliged to remain with their ship during periods of tension, most chose to do so. Many served during the Korean War, the Borneo campaign and the Gulf and Falkland conflicts, and a number of them were awarded campaign medals for their service during these periods. Six received the British Empire Medal. During the hostilities in 1982 in the South Atlantic, two laundrymen were killed when *HMS Coventry* was sunk and *when HMS Sheffield* was struck by an Exocet missile.

The unofficials are now almost exclusively laundrymen. About 100 work onboard Royal Navy ships throughout the world. They are self-employed and the Navy does not undertake any liability for their wages, passage fares or insurance. They work on their own in smaller ships but in teams of up to 12 in aircraft carriers. Only one tailor remains; he serves in *HMS Invincible*. The last barber working onboard left *HMS Illustrious* in 1987, and the last

shoemaker retired on leaving *Ark Royal* in 1994.

On the withdrawal of the British Garrison from Hong Kong, a single fleet-wide contract for the provision of laundry services onboard Royal Naval vessels will be administered from the UK. Most of the existing contractors have notified their intention to tender for the business, so the 60-year-old tradition of Hong Kong Chinese serving the Royal Navy may yet continue into the next century.

THE NAVAL RESERVES IN HONG KONG

For many years the Royal Naval Reserve (RNR) operated in Hong Kong alongside the Royal Navy, and in parallel with its Army and Air Force counterparts, the Hong Kong Regiment (The Volunteers) and the Auxiliary Air Force. The Naval Reserve was made up, until 1967, of two elements: the RNR, who were essentially merchant Navy personnel with some naval training; and the Royal Naval Volunteer Reserve (RNVR), who were civilian volunteers. The RNVR composed the majority of Hong Kong's reserves. The officers were 'yachties' who participated in naval training for

about a fortnight a year and at weekends. The ratings were tough, civilian volunteers from the dockyard and cargo-handling companies. The occasional, and very welcome, telephone engineer or electrician brought specialist skills to the RNVR. Training was usually conducted at designated shoreside establishments named after ships. The Navy called and still do call shore establishments stone frigates, and Hong Kong's was *HMS Cornflower*.

The unofficials. [JSPRS]

111

Laundryman at work. [JSPRS]

HMS Etchingham, *manned by the RNR, October 1966. [Lieutenant Commander GJ May RN]*

Before the Second World War the Royal Navy had several auxiliary patrol vessels that the RNVR manned part-time. The RNVR also ran a minewatching service that specialised in spotting and identifying enemy ships, noting explosions in minefields and, in the case of Hong Kong, assisting in laying mines to be exploded electrically if an enemy ship was identified over the minefield.

The threat from the Japanese in 1941 resulted in calling up RNVR personnel. They performed with bravery and distinction, and their small auxiliary patrol craft operated in support of HMS *Thracian*. They participated in evacuating, under fire, troops from the Kowloon peninsula to Hong Kong Island. The minewatching service assisted in laying mines in Mirs Bay, Lye-Yue-Mun, and in the sea between Lamma and Lantau islands.

During the battle for Hong Kong some auxiliary patrol craft were sunk and others were scuttled to prevent them from falling into enemy hands. These crews joined the survivors of the Royal Navy, creating an informal naval company to assist the Army and the Marines at Wong Nei Chung Gap. Many were killed, some bayoneted by Japanese soldiers, and others drowned when the SS *Lisbon Maru*, transporting them to slave labour in Japan, was torpedoed by an American submarine.

After the war, the RNVR unit took a while to re-establish itself. Returnees from the war and new arrivals helped primarily to rebuild and repair the

112

Royal Hong Kong Yacht Club. The RNVR unit at *HMS Cornflower* returned to its Gloucester Road premises in 1946 to hold drill nights, conduct fortnightly exercises and host dinners. After acquiring a patrol craft, exercises began again with the Royal Navy. Recruits were plentiful and enthusiastic.

The RNVR also experienced occasional confrontations with the People's Liberation Army on outlying islands outside Hong Kong waters. In one incident a RNVR patrol craft strayed too close to some islands on the way to Macau, and was fired upon. In the spirit that attack is the best form of defence, the patrol craft fired back. No obvious damage was caused by either side, and honour was satisfied.

An inshore minesweeper was acquired. Originally built for sweeping the Thames estuary, the vessel was 100 feet long and made of wood to reduce its magnetic field. It had a complement of 20 men and was armed with the standard 40/60 Bofors. The open bridge was comfortable for the watchkeepers, but the mess deck and engine room were very unpleasant in summer.

Officers of the RNVR became 'drivers' in Navy slang, that is; they were qualified for command. Everyone had to join as an Ordinary Seaman unless

1878, the year HMS Tamar first arrived in Hong Kong. [JSPRS]

he had previously held a Royal Navy commission. There was, therefore, an equitable relationship between the officers and the ratings, as the officers had usually joined as ratings. Many RNVR personnel worked for companies in Hong Kong's business hub of Central District, and would meet at work or at play in the famous Wanchai bars of Suzy Wong.

The Hong Kong Government had solely funded the RNVR in Hong Kong, including expensive refits of naval craft, pay and the cost of the shore-side establishment, *HMS Cornflower*. In retrospect, the RNVR made a tactical error in training too closely with the Royal Navy and emphasising its British, rather than Hong Kong, connections. The Hong Kong Volunteers made no such mistake. The regiment was not one of the British Army's, so the Hong Kong Government continued its funding whilst refusing to further finance the RNVR. In 1967 the Ministry of Defence abolished the RNVR, and the minesweeper steamed out of the *Tamar* basin for the last time. The remaining elements of the RNVR were amalgamated with the RNR.

From the demise of the reservists of the Royal Navy there arose the Hong Kong branch of the RNR, which ran a Naval Control of Shipping (NCS) unit. The shore base on Gloucester Road was transferred to three rooms in *HMS Tamar*. Under Commanders Alan Lack and later John Wilson, a strong NCS unit evolved that employed local Hong Kong RNR officers (there were no ratings) and 'augmentees' for naval exercises.

NCS involved a worldwide merchant shipping control organisation that regulated shipping in tense periods and war. The lessons learned in single fast-ship routing and convoy formations from the Second

The Prince of Wales Building in 1979, before the Far East Finance Centre was erected. [Public Records]

nasties were simulated, such as air raids and communication breakdowns. Eventually, convoys would be formed on paper, and paper ships sent on their way. Occasionally there would be a live convoy with real ships and escorts. This posed an organisational challenge, as real convoy conferences and details of speed and zigzag courses needed to be accurately given to merchant ships at sea. For exercises like these the RNR officers were paid a daily rate and a small drill allowance, usually much lower than the civilian rate of pay that they often forewent for the period of the exercise.

In 1981 computerisation of NCS procedures in Hong Kong began, and after two years the Perseus programme, named after the cat belonging to the computer team leader, Lieutenant Julian Stockwin, emerged. At first, senior RNR officers were dubious, and the slow but efficient cards-in-shoe-boxes method was retained until, in 1984, the Hong Kong NCS used Perseus so effectively in an exercise that the American Navy expressed its desire to buy it. The Royal Navy subsequently developed an interest, and within a few years Perseus became the worldwide standard. Lieutenant Julian Stockwin was awarded an MBE for his work.

In 1993 the Ministry of Defence announced that the RNR unit in Hong Kong would close as part of

RFA Fort Austin *comes alongside* West Wall, *1992. [JSPRS]*

the Options for Change initiative, and the door of the training spaces in *HMS Tamar* closed for the last time in early 1994.

The history of the Naval Reserves in Hong Kong has been one of great bravery, sacrifice, technical competence, ingenuity and enthusiasm. The old hands will continue to meet and swing the lantern with their yarns for many years to come.

World War were examined and updated. The NCS would board merchant ships from participating nations in order to obtain details of ships' characteristics, such as cargo, speed, etc., and the instruction of the Master on procedures for tension and war.

The collected information was entered in to a database. Signals from all over the world were added, detailing impending ships' arrivals. During exercises,

JENNY AND THE SIDE PARTY GIRLS

No mention of local Chinese personnel would be complete without the inclusion of the famous side party girls.

A sailor onboard *HMS Dorsetshire* recounted that one of his enduring memories of Hong Kong in 1933 was of a young and very determined Chinese woman climbing up the ship's side by way of the chains to where he was engaged in taking soundings. She wanted the contract for looking after the ship's sides' paintwork. At the time the ship was travelling through the harbour at about ten knots. She was awarded the contract!

The history of side parties goes back to when ships first anchored in the Fragrant Harbour. Side party women worked from walla-wallas and bumboats, and with typical Chinese business acumen were prepared to offer a service to all warships in return for 'arisings' – old wire, rope, canvas, paint and galley swill. When Hong Kong and Wei-Hai-Wei were the Navy's Far East bases, side parties consisting of over 70 women would clean and paint each ship's sides, polish brightwork and carry out other similar jobs from their sampans. An aircraft carrier's sides and bottom line,

The side party girls tackle the aircraft-carrier HMS Centaur *in 1964. [Jenny]*

for example, would be painted in 10 days by these cheerful, energetic women who worked 10 hours a day without complaint.

Each side party had its own harbour territory, and any infringements by another party would prompt

heated disputes. The formidable Mary Soo, all of 4 feet 6 inches tall, with her No. 2 girl Ah Lin and the rest of her side party, worked all the American warships – sometimes as many as 16 at a time during the Vietnam conflict. The Ah Kam Susie Side Party

Jenny and her side party, 1946. [Jenny]

H.M.S. BLACK PRINCE,
c/o G.P.O.

8th March 1946   LONDON.
Hong Kong

It is one of our deepest regrets on leaving for home, that we shall no longer see Jenny & her smiling lasses ('G' morning, Sair) each day.

For cheerfulness, willingness, cleanliness and general niceness Jenny and her charming girls are hard to beat.

G. Gladstone

Captain

Praise from HMS Black Prince in March 1946. [Jenny]

would look after frigates, coastal minesweepers and the Hong Kong flotilla based at *HMS Tamar*, whilst Ah Mee and Ah Moy Side Parties would deal with Royal Fleet Auxilliaries, Commonwealth ships and submarines.

But it was the Jenny Side Party that was the most senior and best known of all. Jenny and her girls worked all the larger British and Commonwealth ships at buoys. There were some 30 Admiralty buoys in 1940, plus those ships that anchored off Green Island. Jenny was the third in a line of Jennys dating from before the First World War. She was born in a sampan at Causeway Bay in 1920, and from an early age worked with her mother. Service Certificates show that her mother (Jenny number two), painted *HM Ships Kent, Carlisle, Cairo* and *Capetown* in 1925.

Jenny's own record is exemplary: her Service Certificates show a list of VG Superiors and, under distinguishing marks, 'Always Smiling'. So many

Jenny meeting the Duke of Edinburgh, 1986. [Jenny]

ships and captains' signatures endorsed Jenny's work that had they been found during the Japanese occupation, her life would have almost certainly been in danger. Jenny hid them in the bilge of her sampan, and she hid the Long Service and Good Conduct Medal presented to her by *HMS Dorsetshire*, in the heel of a shoe for the duration. Governor Sir Murray Maclehose presented Jenny with the British Empire Medal on 27th October 1980. She still keeps in contact with the Royal Navy, using an empty storeroom in the Prince of Wales Barracks as an office.

If Jenny ran the side parties on a contract, Mary 'Gash' took charge of the rubbish. It is reputed that Mary accumulated a considerable fortune from collecting anything and everything discarded by the navies in Hong Kong. Whether it was old mooring lines, wire hawsers, paint tins, wastepaper or aluminium beer cans, Mary recycled any debris she could. Not only was this an example of environmental conservation at its best, it is rumoured that the proceeds paid for her numerous grandchildren to attend the best colleges in Europe and the USA!

Although the side party women were well known for their painting, many remember them – from the most senior admiral to the most recently joined recruit – for their countless acts of generosity and kindness. These included posting a last-minute letter or package to a wife or sweetheart just before a ship sailed, advising on the best places to shop, find a bargain or eat, and visiting sailors sick onshore after their ships had sailed. These women are a cherished link with the past and a reminder of the happy association enjoyed by the Royal Navy and the people of Hong Kong.

Jenny meeting another admirer! 1992. [Jenny]

117

Jenny (left), and Mary Gash at HMS Tamar LEP Farewell Divisions in December 1996. [JSPRS]

THE CHINA FLEET CLUB

The China Fleet Club began its chequered life around the turn of the century. Originally it was no more than a tin hut stuck in the corner of the old Naval Yard, which in those days stretched as far east as the Wanchai district. As the Yard was reduced in size, the tin hut ended up outside the dockyard wall and become known as the Royal Naval Canteen.

By 1920 the Hong Kong Government was planning a reclamation scheme that would include widening Queen's Road. This signaled the end of the canteen, as the site was needed as part of the redevelopment. Nine years passed, during which a considerable amount of land changed hands between the Admiralty and the Hong Kong Government, and a site on the new reclamation was eventually agreed upon for new facilities.

Compensation for the loss of the old site was insufficient to realise the ambitious plan of erecting a six-storey building complete with modern fittings and facilities. The extra funding came from a variety of sources, including a 'whip round' from the men of the China Fleet.

In 1933, Commander-in-Chief China Station, Admiral Sir Howard Kelly, laid the foundation stone of the new building, named The China Fleet Club. One year later it was legally established as a corporation and opened to the men of the fleet. Financially, the club was strong; at the end of the first year of trading the club showed a profit of HK$35,000, and by 1938 its only debt was a small sum still owing on the bank overdraft. All other monies in connection with the construction and furnishing had been paid. This dispelled any doubts about the club's financial independence in the future.

With the rumours of war in 1939, plans for modernisation and extension were shelved in September as the trustees and the management team waited to gauge the effect of the conflict on the operation of the club. Throughout 1940 and most of 1941 the club continued to operate, albeit with smaller profits than in previous years.

When the Japanese started air raids on Hong Kong, the China Fleet Club also went to war. During the battle for Hong Kong the club became, at one time or another, a temporary home for most units of the British Forces in Hong Kong, providing food and shelter for personnel in transit, and assisting with distributing supplies and stores to other areas of the island. For the four years following Hong Kong's surrender to the Japanese Military Forces, the club was the dominion of the Japanese Navy.

Last orders at the bar were called for the occupying forces in August of 1945, and once again the China Fleet Club was in the hands of the Royal Navy. The building had suffered relatively little damage during the occupation; two shell holes and other superficial damage were quickly repaired, and the club was back in business. Renovation and re-decoration continued apace in the following years. The club went from strength to strength, playing host to military personnel from all over the world, particularly during the Korean War in the 1950s and the Vietnam War in the 1960s and 1970s, when sailors of the US fleet poured into Hong Kong for Rest & Recreation.

The famous San Miguel sign on the old China Fleet Club, 1978.
[CFC]

In 1955 the famous *San Miguel* sign, at the time the largest neon-lit advertising board in Hong Kong, was erected on the roof. Ships berthing alongside the north wall at *HMS Tamar* used that sign as a landmark until a *Johnny Walker* sign replaced it in 1960.

The sweeping tide of economic progress propelling Hong Kong into the forefront of world trade brought air conditioning, glassed-in balconies and a host of other improvements. It also meant that

The clubhouse at Saltash, Devon. [CFC]

almost overnight skyscrapers sprouted all around, dwarfing the club. Office space was in huge demand, and the China Fleet Club was on a prime development site. Inevitably, in 1980, a tender was accepted from a local developer to demolish the club and build in its place a 27-storey building that would house, on the bottom nine floors, the China Fleet Club. During construction, the club was relocated to two floors of the Sun Hung Kai Centre and accommodation was available by special arrangement with the Harbour Hotel in Gloucester Road. Thus, club facilities remained uninterrupted.

In May 1985, the Governor of Hong Kong, Sir Edward Youde, opened the new club on exactly the same site as its predecessor. This time, however, there was a marked improvement in the standard of its facilities. It seemed that no expense had been spared: from the elegant marble floors of the entrance area to the real leather chairs in the Kelly Bar, there was evidence everywhere of unbridled luxury. The China Fleet Club had gone up-market. In these boom years in Hong Kong, shrewd investments could generate fortunes overnight. The club's capital reserves soared accordingly.

In London in 1987 plans were drawn up to withdraw the last elements of the China Fleet by 1992. It was envisaged that in five years' time there would be no members of the China Fleet to serve, and under the circumstances it would be difficult to justify the existence of the China Fleet Club. Lengthy discussions culminated in a deal that would provide the Club with HK$160 million and rent-free occupation of the building until the latter part of 1992. Although, subsequently, the naval presence in Hong Kong was extended to the handover to China in 1997, closure plans for the earlier date went ahead. The club continued providing the same standard of service, entertainment and facilities. The proceeds from the sale of the club were channelled back to the UK to provide a new China Fleet Country Club on the banks of the river Tamar at Saltash in Cornwall. Modern facilities there include an 18-hole golf course, an indoor swimming pool, and squash courts and gymnasiums, in addition to the accommodation and entertainment facilities long associated with the China Fleet Club on the other side of the world.

At midnight on 30th November 1992, after a series of farewell parties to mark the closure, the Hong Kong China Fleet Club closed its doors for the last time. For over 50 years the China Fleet Club had been a home away from home for thousands of British sailors. No more would the San Mig flow like the Yangste as sailors forgot the violent storms of the South China Sea, the long sweaty hours in the boiler room, or any of the numerous dirty and unpleasant tasks needed to keep the ships of the China Fleet seaworthy and ready for battle. ∎

PEACOCKS ON PARADE

UPGRADING AND DECOMMISSIONING

The Navy was still performing a significant policing role in the local waters around Hong Kong at the beginning of the 1980s, and it was generally agreed that the old *Ton Class* ships that had been in service around Hong Kong for 30 years needed to be upgraded. Modern replacements were required to fulfil the Navy's role leading to the handover to China in 1997. It was also agreed that under the new Defence Costs Agreement, the ships would be 75% funded, both in terms of construction and future operation, by the Hong Kong Government.

The new ships were specifically designed for patrol duties in Hong Kong waters. Five were built by Hall Russell Limited in Aberdeen, Scotland. With speeds in excess of 25 knots, the 800-ton *Peacock Class* was faster and capable of much greater manoeuvrability than the ships it replaced.

The replacement of the *Ton Class* signalled the end of an era and generated considerable emotion. The last to be de-commissioned was *HMS Wolverton*. She made her final entrance to the basin of *HMS Tamar* in October 1985, flying the traditional 150 foot-long decommissioning pennant. A lone Gurkha piper played a lament on the bridge roof. Farewell to *HMS Wolverton* also meant farewell to Samantha and Scab, possibly the last two sea-dogs to serve with the Navy. A veteran of the *Ton Class* days expressed his feelings in the garrison's *Junk* magazine:

But we, we grizzled veterans of the years, or months, we stand and stare, with a tear in the eye, remembering Old Ships, Old Friends, Old Times. With the passing of the last of the Hong Kong 'Tons' we too die a little, dream a little, remembering the lost days of a class of ship that numbered almost 120, served worldwide and were always handy when a 'gunboat' needed to be sent. Then we return to the present, live for today, get on with the job and look back only when the port has been passed.

HMS Starling, 1996. *[JSPRS]*

HM Ships Plover, *(prior to launch)*, and Starling *during build at Hall Russell Ltd, Aberdeen, April 1983. [Flag Officer Surface Flotilla / FOSF]*

HMS Plover *following her launch by Lady Pamela Youde, wife of His Excellency Sir Edward Youde, Governor of Hong Kong, 1983.* [FOSF]

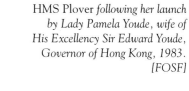

HMS Starling *leaves Portsmouth for the last time, beginning her two-month voyage to Hong Kong in 1984.* [FOSF]

Wolverton ended her days as a floating night club in Hong Kong Harbour. She was opulently refurbished by a local Chinese millionaire and called the Wolverton Club before being renamed the Manhattan Club, and finally Club Venetia. The main service the club offered was reputed to be illegal gambling, and the vessel was raided by the police on several occasions before being gutted by fire following a suspected arson attack. A strange and sad end to a ship with a long and distinguished career.

The first ship to be commissioned in the new class was *HMS Peacock*. She arrived in Hong Kong accompanied by *HMS Plover* in November 1984 to a spectacular welcome:

> *The media were at sea well past the Lye Mun gap to watch the new ships, HM Ships Peacock and Plover, arrived out of a mist escorted by the old patrol craft and Royal Marines on inflatables. The Royal Air Force also paid tribute when Wessex helicopters flew overhead towing a white ensign. As the new vessels entered the harbour other boats sounded their klaxons and fire boats sprayed their hoses high into the air.*

HM Ships *Starling* and *Swallow* arrived in January and April 1985, respectively, and the final ship of the class, *HMS Swift*, was on station on 23rd September 1985. The new ships provided a much

The five Peacocks of the Hong Kong Squadron, 1985. [JSPRS]

123

And then there were three. The last Royal Naval warships to be based in Hong Kong, 1997. [JSPRS]

better living environment for a crew of up to 44 officers and ratings. For the support staff it provided relief from the struggle of maintaining obsolete and aged systems. The mixed manning policy continued and the LEP remained a vital component. The Navy's role, conducting patrols in support of the Marine Police, remained unchanged. This routine required one of the five ships to be at sea at all times, and a weekly patrol cycle came into operation. The ability of the ships to process their own drinking water meant that patrol periods could be extended, whereas the *Tons* had been forced to return for water replenishment every three days.

The upgrade made joint exercises with foreign navies in the region possible, and these could be extended further afield. Deployments as far as Australia, Thailand, Singapore and Indonesia became commonplace. In mid-1988, however, the two newest patrol craft, *HM Ships Swallow* and *Swift*, were withdrawn from the Squadron and sold to Ireland. At the same time, the No. 3 Royal Marine Raiding Squadron was disbanded. ■

Plover dressed overall. In the background is the Royal Hong Kong Yacht Club. [JSPRS]

HMS Peacock in *dry dock, 1989.*
[Lieutenant Commander W Worsley]

A Wessex helicopter from 28 (AC) Squadron prepares to conduct a winch transfer to HMS Plover. [JSPRS]

HMS Plover. *The final ceremonial sunset in Victoria Basin, November 1994. [JSPRS]*

A Wessex helicopter conducting a winch transfer in the South China Sea. [JSPRS]

HMS Starling *with* FPCs, 1995. *[JSPRS]*

The Hong Kong Squadron *leaves Victoria Basin for the last time, November 1994. [JSPRS]*

ILLEGAL IMMIGRATION

THE DILEMMA OF ILLEGAL IMMIGRANTS 1970-1997

The Royal Navy's task in Hong Kong has always been to assist the local government maintain political equilibrium, to be prepared for the outbreak of a limited war in the Eastern hemisphere and to promote good community relations. This triple commitment, however, became overshadowed by the pressing problem of illegal immigrants (IIs as they are known locally). They arrived in huge numbers in the 1960s from Mainland China in the shadow of the Cultural Revolution, and in the late 1970s and 1980s from Vietnam, in the aftermath of the Vietnam War. In their desperate bid to escape persecution, oppression and poverty, the invasion of civilians was composed mostly of young men, but many women, children and babies also joined the bid for freedom. They were often pathetically

The helping hand of the Royal Navy during a humanitarian tragedy. [JSPRS]

ill-equipped for their journey, but were always determined, drawn by the bright lights and the material prosperity of a colony where, some believed, the streets were literally paved with gold.

In one respect these arrivals were nothing new. Refugees had flocked to Hong Kong in 1949 after the Communist victory in China, and again in the 1960s during the Cultural Revolution. The huge difference in the 1970s was the volume. The authorities knew that those caught represented only the tip of the iceberg. In 1978 some 8,000 were caught, but an estimated 28,000 got through. In 1979, 90,000 were caught, but an estimated 108,000 were not. Obviously, such figures posed a threat to the stability of a society already crowded and under pressure to meet housing, health and educational targets.

The influx in the 1970s came by land across the barbed-wire fence erected along the Chinese border from Sha Tau Kok in the east to the marshes of Deep Bay in the west, and by sea from quiet bays and inlets, where a junk or rowing boat could shelter. Some came in home-made rafts, or simply swam or waded across the mud flats at low tide. Shark encounters were common, but the IIs were prepared to risk all to reach the promised land.

To counter this threat to the stability of the colony, the Navy mobilised about 700 officers and men, half of them LEP, to patrol the eastern and western approaches to Hong Kong. The work was first undertaken by the five-ton-class converted minesweepers and by the ex-dockyard tug, *Clare*, which stopped and searched suspicious-looking vessels, such as those not displaying the required

Vietnamese refugees fill a landing craft en route to detention. [JSPRS]

lights. It was difficult to distinguish between a junk returning home with its holds full of fish and one that might be carrying a less legal cargo, so the task demanded a certain feel and flair and the exercise of intuition, built up over several months of experience.

When a boat carrying IIs had been identified,

130

These frail vessels often proved tragically inadequate, and the patrols would regularly have to pluck from the sea the bodies of those who had died in the attempt to escape.

A new dimension to this nautical game of hide and seek came with the introduction of speed. Those immigrants able to pay the often exorbitant price (approximately HK$2,000 in 1980), were transported from Macau across the South China Sea in high-powered speedboats that could easily outrun the patrol craft. The Navy's answer to this challenge was its two 50-knot SRN 6 hovercraft and the 40-knot fast patrol craft *HMS Scimitar*. Working closely with the patrol craft on duty and with the vessels of the Marine Police, these could easily dash to the area of a sighting and pursue the quarry. They were frequently helped by helicopters flown by the Royal Air Force and Army Air Corps and fitted with the xenon-arc 65-million candle-power searchlight, Nite Sun. When trained on the speedboat driver, it dazzled and disorientated him, causing him either to lose his sense of direction and go round in circles, or to cut his engines and give up the game. Occasionally a driver would lose control completely and smash himself, his boat and its occupants to pieces on the foreshore. From a crash at such speed there were usually few survivors.

Vietnamese refugees being transferred to holding camps by naval ferry. [JSPRS]

the patrol craft came alongside and a Chinese-speaking member of the crew would address the occupants by loud-hailer. They were searched and made to sit on deck in groups under armed guard. Having been given something to eat and drink, they were handed over to the Marine Police to be repatriated.

Much of the action took place at night, as for obvious reasons most immigrants preferred to make their escape bids under the cover of darkness.

A particular problem for the Navy was that many of the craft involved were little more than rowing boats with a sail, quite open to the elements and so small as scarcely to register on a radar screen.

Also involved in this battle of wits were the fast boats, more commonly known as Rigid Raiders, of the Royal Marines of *No. 3 Marine Raiding Squadron*. This job demanded great physical resilience, for these craft provided little protection from wet and bumpy conditions while the Marines lay in wait night after night in quiet bays, for the chase to begin. When it did, their role was often to join with the launches of the Hong Kong Marine Police in forming a moving funnel shape down which the speed boat was driven, with the objective of diverting it from its intended course. Although by day the Marines were accustomed to stopping and boarding junks, this was impossible at night with boats operating at high speed. Consequently the aim was either to force the speedboat out to sea where it would eventually run out of fuel, or into the waiting net in the harbour. As the campaign continued, it was this type of action that slashed the previously high success rate of the speedboats in the early days.

Towards the end of the 1980s the situation altered radically. The flood of Chinese IIs became a stream, then a trickle. A mere handful of immigrants attempted to enter the colony weekly. The Hong Kong government had previously operated the Touch Base Policy: when an II reached urban Hong Kong, he was given an identity card that ensured

Illegal immigrants apprehended by a Duty Patrol Craft. [JSPRS]

his right to stay. This was introduced to prevent criminal elements from operating black-market or blackmail rackets. When the government abandoned the Touch Base Policy it meant that refugees were no longer automatically issued identity cards. Employers engaging staff without one

were subject to a heavy fine. An additional factor in the decrease of IIs was undoubtedly the attitude of China, which initiated measures to prevent its citizens from escaping. China deployed the 42nd Army, some 20,000-strong, along the land frontier, and applied pressure on the leaders of communes to

SRN 6 *hovercraft, based in Stonecutters Island.*
[Kathleen Harland]

ensure that their members did not make any abrupt departures. When the Touch Base policy was abandoned in 1980, total arrests of Chinese IIs dropped sharply from about 90,000 a year to 10,000.

The decline in Chinese IIs meant that the reinforcements originally called in to deal with the situation could be sent home. *Scimitar* returned to the United Kingdom in 1981, and the hovercraft unit ceased to be operational in April 1982, before being disbanded in September of that year. Nevertheless, the lights of Hong Kong continued to beckon, and Hong Kong Squadron ships regularly caught small numbers of IIs well into 1997. ◼

HMS Scimitar *in action. [Kathleen Harland]*

A smuggler, with his contraband of air conditioners, gives the Air Force a nervous wave. [JSPRS]

SEIZING SMUGGLERS AND SAVING SOULS

FURTHER CHALLENGES

During the 1980s Vietnamese refugees sought asylum in Hong Kong at an ever-increasing rate. In early June 1989, 1,103 Vietnamese refugees arrived in a single day. The Navy's role was to assist the Marine Police in rounding up the ramshackle boats, which were generally barely seaworthy, and transporting the refugees (a new role for the Royal Navy Ferries), to the Green Island reception area. Many of the Vietnamese arriving in Hong Kong came from the southern provinces of China, where they had been living for up to 10 years. They made the treacherous journey fuelled by rumours that Hong Kong and countries such as the USA, Canada and Australia were willing to provide asylum. Such rumours were of course unsubstantiated, and Hong Kong was left with the problem of providing holding facilities prior to repatriation to Vietnam.

Three smuggling vessels break from their contraband supplier when observed by the Security Services. [JSPRS]

135

Police Special Boat Unit and naval personnel bring two captured Tai Feis (Big Flyers), complete with stolen cars, into Victoria Basin, 1992. [JSPRS]

As the social and political environment in the region continued to change ahead of the handover, so the nature of local patrol work adapted. The number of illegal immigrants running the gauntlet continued to decrease, and with the imposition of tougher sentences, numbers of illegal immigrants caught daily averaged 35 by the time of the Tiananmen Square Incident in 1989.

The impending handover date inevitably had a significant affect not only on the operation of the Navy during this period but on the Garrison as a whole. The integrity of Hong Kong waters had to be maintained until 30th June 1997, but it was also necessary to put into effect a general scaling down of the overall force levels. For the officers and ratings involved it continued to be a very hectic and demanding time.

Increasing prosperity amongst some of the Mainland Chinese population meant that there was no shortage of money or customers for high-price items from Hong Kong. Smuggling became an increasingly hi-tech and lucrative trade, with smugglers operating in teams using radio-linked fishing junks, decoys and multi-engined high-speed boats. The largest were capable of achieving around 75 knots, and this led to some exciting chases by the Squadron's Fast Pursuit Craft.

In fact, the early 1990s were an extremely busy time for the Squadron. A patrol report from *HMS Peacock* in 1991 over a 12-day period included the arrest of 20 sampans, four speedboats and a junk carrying three stolen cars. The haul of illicit cargo included 130 TV sets, six vehicles, some HK$300,000 in cash and 40 illegal immigrants. Lieutenant Commander Carey, captain of *HMS Peacock*, describes an incident on the night of 14th October 1992:

. . . we were conducting a joint anti-smuggling operation with the Hong Kong Police, when a group of Tai Feis [fast speedboats] configured for smuggling were spotted loitering south of Kau Yi Chau island, to the west of Hong

Captured high-powered Tai Feis with stolen cars, in Victoria Basin, 1992. [JSPRS]

Anti-II operations. HMS Starling *with her Fast Pursuit Craft.* [JSPRS]

*The Royal Marines,
equipped with Fast Pursuit Craft . . .*

. . . board a greenhull . . .

. . . search the vessel . . .

. . . and check documentation. [JSPRS]

Kong Island. Two Fast Pursuit Craft [FPC] were launched from *Peacock* to investigate and attempt interception. A Royal Navy rating from one of the FPCs jumped aboard one of the *Tai Feis* as it tried to speed away and attempted to cut the fuel supply to the 10 metre vessel's five large outboard engines to immobilise it. In the course of this action he was subjected to a series of attacks by two of the four-man crew wielding weapons, during which he received bruises and lacerations. By this time, the *Tai Fei* was making 50-60 knots heading south out of Hong Kong waters. As the attacks on the rating continued, he felt so threatened that he drew his 9mm pistol and fired 3 shots in self-defence at his assailants. As a result, one of his attackers received a bullet wound in the arm and the other was wounded in the leg. Both men jumped into the sea, while the remaining two on the *Tai-Fei* were overpowered and detained.

The Royal Marines of 3 Raiding Squadron, equipped with Fast Pursuit Craft, were employed on anti-smuggling duties until they were disbanded in mid-1988.
Subsequently, Royal Marines with FPCs embarked in the Peacocks to continue this valuable work. [JSPRS]

An FPC jostles with a Tai Fei during a demonstration for Navy Days, 1996. [Captain Simon Scott RM]

As a training exercise, LS Matt Fisher of HMS Plover leaps onboard a Police Tai Fei at 55 knots, 1996. [Captain Simon Scott RM]

3 Raiding Squadron Royal Marines, 1988. [JSPRS]

A Royal Marine about to abseil
down the Prince of Wales Building. [JSPRS]

Royal Marines in Hong Kong harbour in 1996. Construction of the new Convention Centre, the venue for the 1997 handover ceremonies, can be seen in the background. [JSPRS]

A Chinese Customs Patrol Vessel. [JSPRS]

Chinese customs police returning a Fast Pursuit Craf that had inadvertently drifted into Chinese waters, to its rightful owner, 1986. [Trevor Hollingsbee]

A Chinese Patrol Vessel exercising its right of passage through Hong Kong's territorial waters en route to its base in northern Mirs Bay. [JSPRS]

The newest Chinese Customs Patrol Vessel, nicknamed the 'Bat boat'. [JSPRS]

USS Enterprise, 1993. [JSPRS]

HMCS Kootenay, 1990. [Trevor Hollingsbee]

Australian frigates alongside South Wall, 1994. [JSPRS]

USS Narragansett, tender to a visiting American nuclear submarine. [JSPRS]

SEARCH AND RESCUE AND DISASTER RELIEF

Other operational tasks were Search and Rescue (SAR), where the patrol craft provided the region's only deep sea capability. The longer range of the *Peacock Class* meant that the Navy could provide a much more effective SAR capability.

In a typical incident in December, 1986 *HMS Swift* intercepted an SOS distress call from the 2,000-ton Taiwanese freighter *MV Kwang Ta No.2*. Her cargo of scrap metal and engine parts had shifted in heavy seas and she was listing up to 60 degrees to starboard. Despite considerable risk to the members of the boarding party, all the crew, except for the Captain who elected to stay with his ship, were transferred by Sea Raider to *Swift*, and a line was passed to conduct a 200-mile tow to Hong Kong waters.

Disaster relief is another common feature of life in the Hong Kong Squadron. Typically, the Territory is affected by five or six tropical storms every year and lies adjacent to an active earthquake zone. In August 1991 an offshore oilfield support barge with 195 men on board capsized 65 miles southeast of Hong Kong in tumultuous seas whipped up by

HMS Swift. *Search and Rescue operations with the Government Flying Service.*
[The Government Flying Service]

Typhoon Fred. *HM Ships Plover* and *Peacock*, together with helicopters of the RAF and Hong Kong Auxiliary Air Force, conducted the rescue operation in storm-force conditions. Eventually 173 of those on board were rescued, 16 bodies were recovered and six were posted missing presumed dead. An RAF Flight Lieutenant and four men from the Royal Navy received awards for bravery.

In 1971, Typhoon Rose hit the Colony. Around 50 ships went aground or were otherwise wrecked, and the Hong Kong Squadron was soon busy rescuing seamen from their stricken vessels. This included the US supply ship, USS Regulus, which went aground and broke her back on Green Island (left). The Commodore-in-Charge, who at the time had authority over all Commonwealth and American ships in the event of a typhoon, had ordered all ships to sea to ride out the worst of the storm. Regulus's Commanding Officer, Captain Nelson, had elected to return to anchor in the shelter of Green Island. The Squadron subsequently rescued 230 crew members, beefsteak and ice-cream. Needless to say, the Squadron ate well that month! [Captain David Whitehead]

A merchantman aground in residential Cheung Chau after severe typhoon, 1983. [JSPRS]

The Taiwanese freighter Kwang Ta No.2 under tow by HMS Swift, 1986. [JSPRS]

147

Navy divers from the Hong Kong Squadron assisted with emergencies at Kai Tak International Airport, 1985. [JSPRS]

HMS Plover *tackling the blazing* Seastar *in April 1992. Firefighters battled the fire for 36 hours before bringing it under control. [JSPRS]*

Firefighters after beating the blaze onboard Seastar. *[JSPRS]*

Seastar's *Master, Mr Ho Sheng, and his crew salute* Plover *and her Captain, Lieutenant Commander Ian MacKenzie. [JSPRS]*

The Hydrographic Survey Fleet in Hong Kong. [JSPRS]

HMS Norfolk, HMS Boxer *and* RFA Olwen *during Orient 1992. [JSPRS]*

HMY Britannia arriving at HMS Tamar, 1992. [JSPRS]

HMS Exeter, 1996. [JSPRS]

RECLAMATION

In April 1993 the Navy's last remaining coastal watching station in Hong Kong, and indeed the world, closed down. The Tai-O Coastal Watching Station was one of five built shortly after World War II to monitor shipping transiting to and from the Chinese mainland. Five naval ratings worked for six weeks at a time in the post, and were helicoptered in with their provisions. Double-linked barbed-wire surrounded the 200-square-metre site, and guard dogs patrolled the perimeter. Tai-O was the last station to help provide information on ships entering Hong Kong waters. Following the closing ceremony, the buildings were handed over to the Hong Kong Government.

HMS Tamar, in Central, could no longer resist the tide of history. The land on which it had stood had simply become too valuable for defence use. At 2017 on 17th May 1993, over a hundred years after an earlier governor had first asked the Royal Navy to vacate, the White Ensign was lowered for the last time in the 5th *HMS Tamar*. The men of the Hong Kong Squadron certainly regretted the loss of the most centrally placed base in the world, but continued to use the basin right up until November

HMS Trenchant *and RFA Diligence, 1995. [JSPRS]*

1995, when the first barge-load of landfill was emptied into it. What had been the fifth *HMS Tamar* now became the Prince of Wales Barracks, and soldiers in combats replaced the white uniforms of sailors on the main gate. The land the Government regained was expected to sell for HK$35 billion, so the provision of a new base, the sixth *HMS Tamar* on Stonecutters Island, costing HK$1.5 billion, was a bargain.

The Royal Navy's link with Central continued, however. As the new base on Stonecutters Island had no mess facilities, the Prince of Wales Building remained home for the 600 men and women who

made up the complements of *HMS Tamar* and the Hong Kong Squadron.

In 1994 *HMS Tamar* ceased to be an independent command responsible to the Commander-in-Chief Fleet. In May of that year the Army Commander British Forces Hong Kong was given full command of all three services, and in July the post of Captain-in-Charge was abolished. *HMS Tamar* became a Commander's command, whilst the Navy's pride was salvaged to some extent by the appointment of a Captain (later Commodore) as Chief of Staff and Deputy to the Commander British Forces. ■

The new HMS Tamar and naval basin on Stonecutters Island, opened in 1993. [JSPRS]

Stonecutters "Island," is now part of the mainland. The future Chinese naval base can be seen under construction in the foreground, with HMS Tamar to the right. [JSPRS]

HMS Ark Royal, Outback '88. [JSPRS]

With Victoria Basin filled in, the new site, called East Tamar, will provide the setting for the British Farewell Ceremony on 30th June 1997. [JSPRS]

Several more reclamation phases are anticipated. By 2015 the waterfront may well look like this, with the new buildings depicted in white. The Prince of Wales Building is in the centre in grey. [JSPRS]

The Governor, Chris Patten, inspects the naval guard of the sailors from HMS Trenchant during the Liberation Day Parade in August 1995. [JSPRS]

END OF AN ERA

156 YEARS OF SERVICE

The close connection between the people of Hong Kong and the Royal Navy, and the British Services in general, was clearly demonstrated at the last combined Navy and Garrison Open Day, held in November 1996. A record 45,000 people swarmed onto Stonecutters Island to witness a variety of military displays and to see the ships and other military hardware for the last time. Significantly, the event raised HK$1.5 million for the LEP Trust, established to assist with the welfare of ex-LEP and their families following the handover.

In December 1996 hundreds of families and former naval servicemen came to *HMS Tamar* to witness an emotional last Naval Divisions for the LEP in Hong Kong. The parade provided an opportunity for the ships' companies of *HMS Tamar* and of *HM Ships Peacock* and *Plover* to applaud the hard work and loyalty of the LEP during the

Margaret Thatcher, later Baroness Thatcher, who in December 1984 signed the Sino-British Joint Declaration determining Hong Kong's future. [JSPRS]

more than 90-year association with the Navy. Jenny Side Party BEM and Mary Gash, much loved figures from the Royal Navy's past, turned up to witness Divisions and reminisce about the days when the LEP Division had numbered over a thousand and there had always been a ship's side to paint.

On 11th April 1997 *HMS Tamar* decommissioned and the White Ensign was lowered ashore in the Far East for the last time. The First Sea Lord, Admiral Sir Jock Slater and the last Governor of Hong Kong, Christopher Patten, took the salute as over 200 sailors marched past, out of *Tamar's* gates with their 1878 foul anchors, and into history. The Governor said: 'You do not leave in the darkness, nor in the pomp of pride, but in the quiet dignity of men and women who have done their job well.' By coincidence, it was 100 years to the day since *HMS Tamar* took over as Receiving Ship from *HMS Victor Emmanuel.*

On Stonecutters Island a new naval base has sprung up, paid for by the Hong Kong taxpayer,

Gun Salute from the Bull's Nose. Once reclamation of Victoria Basin began, salutes were given by the Patrol Craft in the harbour. [JSPRS]

RFA Sir Percivale, *the logistic support ship tasked with the final withdrawal of essential and classified stores from Hong Kong.* [FOSF]

HMS Chatham, *the Batch III Type 22 frigate, will be used to control military operations in Hong Kong during the final months of British sovereignty.* [FOSF]

HMY Britannia, *in one of its last official visits before decommissioning, will provide the backdrop for the farewell ceremony on 30th June 1997.* [FOSF]

(Above) Lieutenant Commander Will Worsley, Senior Officer Afloat Hong Kong Squadron, greets Major General Liu Zhen Wu, future Chinese Garrison Commander. [JSPRS]

which will house the Navy of the People's Liberation Army's Hong Kong Squadron, and the sixth *HMS Tamar* will become the government dockyard.

One hundred and fifty-six years after Commodore Bremer first claimed Hong Kong for Britain, the Royal Navy's chapter in the history of the Far East is coming to a close. Task Groups will still deploy to exercise with friendly nations, particularly those of the Five Power Defence Agreement, but 30th June 1997 truly marks the end of an era. Nowhere in the world is the old adage that trade follows the flag more true than on the China coast. Nowhere in the world has the security inspired by the flag brought greater wealth and success than in Hong Kong. The 156-year marriage of the White Ensign of the Royal Navy with the Red Dragon of China has truly been a major force in shaping the prosperity of the Pacific Rim. ■

30th June 1997 will see the Royal Navy's final sunset on a British Hong Kong.
The Navy has been the guardian and protector here for many years, in a more direct
manner than anywhere else in the world. From the congested waters of Victoria Harbour to
the choppy, muddy seas of Mirs Bay, the Royal Navy has provided deterrence, support and
protection – perhaps the last of this sort of extended, permanent, patrolling presence that the
UK will ever require East of Suez. [Lieutenant Commander G Tilsey RN]

HMS Beaver, *passing the Hong Kong Convention Centre in May 1997 [JSPRS]*

HMS Beaver, *moored alongside the Victoria Basin reclamation [JSPRS]*

RFA Fort George, *arriving to remove stores and equipment [JSPRS]*

RFA Sir Percivale, *berthing at Stonecutters Naval Base [JSPRS]*

HMS Tamar, *the decommissioning of Hong Kong's last Royal Naval Base [JSPRS]*

HMS Tamar, *the last moments whilst the White Ensign flew in Hong Kong [JSPRS]*

Lowering the White Ensign [JSPRS]

HMS Tamar's Ship's Bell [JSPRS]

The First Sea Lord Admiral Sir Jock Slater receives the folded ensign [JSPRS]

The First Sea Lord and The Governor Chris Patten sign limited first editions of
White Ensign ~ Red Dragon [JSPRS]

Jenny Side Party gives her approval to the book [JSPRS]

The book launch of White Ensign ~ Red Dragon in April 1997 [JSPRS]

BIBLIOGRAPHY

Anon, *Hongkong Volunteer Defence Corps in the Battle for Hong Kong, Dec 1941* (Hong Kong, 1953)

Bannister, T. R., *A History of the External Trade of China 1834-81* (London, 1932)

Belcher, E., *A Voyage Round the World* (London, 1983)

Bell, Major M., *Narrative of the British Wars in China* (India, 1881)

Bernard, W. D., *Narrative of the Voyage of the 'Nemesis'* (London, 1844)

Blake, C., *Charles Elliot* (London, 1960)

Bruce P., *Lyemun Barracks, 140 Years of Military History* (Hong Kong, 1987)

Cameron, N., *Hong Kong: The Cultured Pearl* (Hong Kong, 1978)

　　An Illustrated History of Hong Kong (Hong Kong, 1991)

Carew, T., *Fall of Hong Kong* (London)

Chambers, G., *Eastern Waters, Eastern Winds* (Hong Kong)

Chiu, T. N., *The Port of Hong Kong; A Survey of its Development* (Hong Kong, 1973)

Cole, B. D., *Gunboats and Marines* (Delaware, 1983)

Conways All the World's Fighting Ships 1860-1905 (London)

Cree, E., *The Voyages of Edward H. Cree, R.N. as Related in his Private Journals 1837-56*, ed. Michael Levien (Exeter, 1981)

Critchley, M., *British Warships since 1945* (Liskeard, 1980s)

Donnison, F.S.V., *British Military Administration in the Far East 1943-46* (London, 1956)

Elliot, C., *A Plan for the Formation of a Maritime Militia* (London, 1852)

Endacott, G. B., *Government and People in Hong Kong 1841-1962* (Hong Kong, 1964)

　　A History of Hong Kong (Hong Kong, 1973)

Fay, P. W., *The Opium War 1840-42* (Chapel Hill, 1975)

Fox, G., *British Admirals and Chinese Pirates* (London, 1940)

Gillingham, P., *At the Peak: Hong Kong between the Wars* (Hong Kong, Macmillan, 1983)

Graham, G. S., *The China Station: War and Diplomacy 1830-60* (Oxford, 1978)

Grenfell, R., *Main Fleet to Singapore* (London, 1951)

Hall, Captain W. H. (R.N.), *The 'Nemesis' in China, with a complete account of the Colony of Hong Kong* (London, 1846)

Halpern, P. G., *A Naval History of World War I* (London)

Harland, K., *The Royal Navy in Hong Kong Since 1841* (Liskeard, 1985)

Hayes, J., *The Hong Kong Region 1850-1911* (Connecticut, 1977)

Hibbert, C., *The Dragon Wakes, China and the West 1793-1911*, (London, 1970)

Hill, J. R., (ed), *The Oxford Illustrated History of the Royal Navy* (Oxford, 1995)

Hong Kong Government, Museum of Art, *The Pearl River in the Nineteenth Century* (Hong Kong, 1981)

Horstman, C., *The China Coast: Ships, Ports and People* (Hong Kong, 1980)

Hutcheon, R., *South China Morning Post: The First Eighty Years* (Hong Kong, 1983)

Inglis, B., *The Opium War* (London, 1976)

Janes Fighting Ships, various volumes between 1898 and 1996/97

Keppel, H., *A Sailors Life* (London, 1899)

Keswick, M. (ed.), *The Thistle and the Jade: 150 Years of Jardine Matheson* (London, 1982)

Lindsay, O., *At the Going Down of the Sun* (London, 1981)

　　The Lasting Honour: The Fall of Hong Kong 1941 (London, 1978)

Miller, H., *Pirates of the Far East* (London)

Morris, D., *Cruisers of the Royal and Commonwealth Navies* (Liskeard)

Morris, J., *Building Hong Kong, with an essay by Jan Morris* (Hong Kong, 1989)

Ochterlony, J., *The Chinese War: An Account of the Operations* (London, 1844)

Oxley, Lieutenant Colonel D. H., *Victoria Barracks 1842-1979* (Hong Kong, 1979)

Preston, A. and Major J., *Send a Gunboat!* (London, 1967)

Preston, A., *Battleships of World War I* (London)

Singer, A., *The Lion and the Dragon* (London, 1992)

Smith, J. S., *Matilda* (Hong Kong, 1988)

Thorne, C., *The Far Eastern War* (London, 1985)

Tolley, K., *Yangtse Patrol* (Annapolis, 1971)

Waley, A., *The Opium War Through Chinese Eyes* (London, 1958)

Warner, J., *Hong Kong a Hundred Years Ago* (Hong Kong, 1970)

　　Fragrant Harbour (Hong Kong, 1976)

Welsey-Smith, P., *Unequal Treaty, 1898-1997* (Hong Kong, 1980)

Welsh, F., *A History of Hong Kong* (London, 1993)

Wilshire, T., *Hong Kong – Last Prize of the Empire* (Hong Kong, 1996)

　　Old Hong Kong (Hong Kong, 1996)

KEY TO CHRONOLOGY OF SHIPS

I do not claim that this chronology is by any means definitive. It attempts to list most of the ships that have seen service in the Colony and its surrounding seas, but it has not been possible to mention every Royal Naval warship that has visited; it concentrates on those ships which have either been based in, or made a number of visits to, Hong Kong. Where information has been vague, incomplete, or contradictory, intelligent guesswork has been applied. Where data is omitted, it is because suitable sources have not been found.

Date	Approximate date of first appearance in Hong Kong
Name	Ship's name at time of service in Hong Kong
Tons	Tonnage as appropriate at time of service in Hong Kong
Armament	Number and calibre of guns mounted [eg 2x7 indicated two 7 inch callibre guns, [20pdr indicates a 20 pound ball]
Sp	Designed speed (– indicates unknown or a sail ship)
Channel	Channel Fleet
CS	Cruiser Squadron
LCS	Light Cruiser Squadron
FS	Frigate Squadron
SS	Screw Steamer
SMS	Sein Majestts Schiff (WW I German warship)
KMS	Kriegsmarine Schiff (WW II German warship)
HEICo	Honourable East India Company
HIJMS	His Imperial Japanese Majesty's Ship
Home	Home Fleet
TT	Torpedo Tube
Pl	Planes

DATE	NAME	TONS	ARMAMENT	SP	OUTLINE OF SERVICE HISTORY
1834	Andromache	709	28	-	Sloop built 1832; carried Lord and Lady Napier and their two daughters to Macau
1834	Imogene	-	-	-	Frigate
1834	Louisa	-	-	-	Cutter; Battle of the Bogue 1834
1839	Larne	-	15	-	Sloop
1839	Volage	-	28	-	Frigate; Battle of the Junks 1839; Battle of Chuen Pee
1839	Hyacinth	-	18	-	Frigate; Battle of the Junks 1839; Battle of Chuen Pee
1839	Pearl	-	-	-	Battle of the Junks
1839	Cambridgeshire	-	22	-	Battle of Chuen Pee
1839	Rambler	835	-	10	Composite gun vessel completed as a survey ship; surveyed HK waters
1840	Wellesley	1746	74	-	3rd Rate built 1815; Chuen Pee forts 1841
1840	Melville	-	74	-	3-decker; Battle of Chuen Pee; later became a hospital hulk
1840	Blonde	-	-	-	Frigate; exchange of fire Amoy 1840
1841	Sulphur	-	-	-	Surveyed HK waters
	Minden	-	-	-	Hospital Ship; Store Ship 1846
1841	Nemesis	1128	46	-	HEICo armed steamer; see Agincourt, 1846; see Albatross, 1848
1841	Blenheim	1822	74	-	3rd Rate ship of the line built 1813; converted to screw ship with 5x50 pdr 1837; signature of Chuen Pee Convention 1841; scrapped 1865
1842	Cornwallis	1809	74	-	3rd Rate ship of the line built 1813; signature of Treaty of Nanking 1842; converted to screw steamer 1855; scrapped 1857
1842	Dido	734	18	-	Sailing sloop built 1836; in which Admiral Keppel & Brooke enlisted the support of Raja Muda Hashim of Kuching for the suppression of piracy 1842; with SS Phlegethon, Brooke's own Jolly Bachelor, and some 400 Dyaks in canoes dealt with the Sareba and Sekrang forts 1842; sold 1903
1845	Samarang	500	28	-	Sailing sloop built 1822; failed to gain admission to Japan 1845; scrapped 1883
1846	Agincourt	1747	74	-	3rd rate built 1817; with Iris, Ringdove, Hazard, Daedalus, Royalist, & Spiteful and HEICo's Phlegethon, & Pluto, bombarded Brunei Town to impress the Sultan's court with the importance of suppressing piracy 1846; with Vestal, Daedalus, Vixen, Cruiser & Wolverine and HEICo's Pluto & Nemesis, broke the boom and stormed the pirate chief Usop's stronghold at Marudu Bay; 1846; sold 1884
1846	Ringdove	-	-	-	See Agincourt, 1846;
1846	Spiteful	1054	6	-	Paddle sloop built 1842; see Agincourt, 1846; sold 1883
1846	Vestal	913	26	-	6th Rate built 1833; see Agincourt, 1846; scrapped 1882
1846	Daedalus	1083	46	-	5th Rate built 1826; see Agincourt, 1846; sold 1911
1846	Vixen	1054	6	-	Paddle sloop built 1941; bombarded the house of the pirate chief Usop in Brunei 1846; see Agincourt, 1846; sold 1862
1846	Cruiser	-	-	-	Brig; see Agincourt, 1846
1846	Wolverine	-	-	-	Brig; see Agincourt, 1846
1846	Hazard	431	18	-	Sailing sloop built 1837; her arrival at Kuching saved Brooke's life after the massacre of Raja Muda Hashim and 13 of his brothers and relatives; scrapped 1866
1846	Iris	-	-	-	Frigate; see Agincourt, 1846
1848	Maeander	1221	44	-	Sailing 5th Rate built 1840; conveyed Brooke to the new colony of Labuan 1848; wrecked 1870
1848	Albatross	-	-	-	With Royalist & HEICo Nemesis stormed pirate Sarebas and Sekrang stronghold in Kaluka river for which Admiralty Court granted prize money of £20,700, made up of £10,000 for the estimated 500 pirates killed and £10,700 for the estimated 2140 pirates who escaped
1848	Royalist	-	-	-	See Albatross, 1848; see Agincourt, 1846
1849	Pilot	-	16	-	Sailing brig; in action with pirates in Bias Bay; sold 1862
1849	Amazon	1078	46	-	5th Rate built 1821; following the location of part of Shap-ng-Tsai's pirate fleet near Hainan by the chartered P&O's Canton, HM Ships Amazon, Inflexible & Columbine and HEICo Phlegethon, sank Shap's fleet 1849; later, joined by Fury & Hastings from HK, they completely destroyed Shap's main fleet and base in Bias Bay for which the Vice-Admiralty Court in HK awarded a bounty of £15,000 for the Bias operation and £6,200 for the Hainan one, 1849; sold 1863
1849	Inflexible	112	26	-	Paddle sloop built 1845; see Amazon, 1849; sold 1864
1849	Columbine	4921	8	-	Sloop built 1826; see Amazon, 1849; defeated remains of Shap's pirate fleet sinking some 38 junks, with some 1,200 cannon and 3,000 crew 1849; 12 gun brig 1849; coal hulk 1854; sold 1842
1842	Phlegethon				Chartered HEICo iron paddle vessel built 1839; see Dido, see Amazon, Columbine, 1849
1849	Hastings	1764	60	-	Ex-HEICo 3rd Rate built 1819; see Amazon, 1849; converted to screw 1855; sold 1886
1849	Fury	1124	6	-	Paddle sloop built 1845; see Amazon, Columbine, 1849; sold 1864
1849	Medea	833	4	-	Paddle sloop built 1833; came upon remains of Shap's pirate fleet and finding it of overwhelming strength, returned to HK for reinforcements 1849
1854	Encounter	953	14	-	Screw corvette built 1846; at Shanghai during Battle of the Muddy Flats, 1854; at Canton 1856; scrapped 1866
1855	Rattler	1112	6	-	Screw sloop built 1843; together with USS Phowatan, defeated a large pirate fleet off Goalan Island, about 100 miles SW HK the Kuhlan monument is now in Happy Valley Cemetery
1855	Bittern	-	-	-	Sloop
1857	Inflexible	1122	6	-	Paddle sloop built 1845; took Commissioner Yeh Ming-chen to Calcutta 1857; sold 1864
1859	Cormorant	670	4	-	Screw gun vessel built 1855; sunk in action in China 1859
1859	Plover	232	2	-	Screw gunboat built 1856; sunk in action in China 1859
1859	Jaseur, Lee	301	2	-	Screw gunboats built 1857; sunk in action in China 1859
1859	Princess Charlotte	2443	104	-	1st Rate built 1825; Receiving Ship HK; sold 1875
1861	Calcutta	2299	84	-	Sailing ship of the line built 1831; sold 1908
1868	Rattler	1280	5x40 pdr	10	Wooden screw sloop built 1864; wrecked on China station 1868
1868	Meeanee	-	-	-	Ex-80 gun 3rd Rate Hospital Ship sometimes used as markboat for rowing regattas
1870	Wivern	2751	-	-	Ex-Coast Defence Ship built 1865; Guardship HK c.1870; later distilling ship and workshop
1871	Forester	232	2	-	Screw gunboat built 1855; lost in typhoon 1871
1872	Swinger	430	2x64	9	Composite gunboat built 1872; sold 1924

DATE	NAME	TONS	ARMAMENT	SP	OUTLINE OF SERVICE HISTORY
1875	Waterwitch	1230	2x7, 2x20	8	Iron armoured gunboat built 1867; engined with experimental jet propulsion turbines which proved almost useless; surveyed HK
1875	Moorhen	455	2x64pdr	10	Composite gunboat built 1875; sold 1888
1875	Excellent	2289	104	-	Ex-Queen Charlotte sailing 1st Rate ship of the line built 1810; sold 1892
1875	Inflexible	1122	6	-	Paddle sloop built 1845; sold 1884
1875	Victor Emmanuel	3087	91	-	Screw ship of the line built 1855; receiving ship; sold 1899
1878	Vigilant	-	-	-	Paddle despatch boat
1878	Lapwing, Curler	1870	1x7, 2x40pdr	10	Wooden gun vessels built 1869; sold c1885
1878	Growler	576	1x7, 1x64pdr	9	Composite gun vessel built 1867; sold 1887
1878	Magpie	755	1x7, 2x40pdr	10	Wooden gun vessel built 1868; sold 1885
1878	Shannon	5760	2x10, 7x9pdr	12	Armoured cruiser built 1877; sold 1899
1878	Diamond	1970	14x64pdr	12	Wooden screw corvette built 1873; sold 1889
1878	Ruby	2120	12x64pdr	12	Composite screw corvette built 1877; sold 1921
1878	Charybdis	2231	21	-	Screw corvette built 1859; scrapped 1884
1879	Kestrel	610	1x7, 1x64pdr	10	Frolic-class wooden gun vessel built 1872; destroyed pirate base at Tunku, British North Borneo 1879; sold 1888
1878	Audacious	5909	10x9, 4x6	14	Central battery ironclad built 1870; scrapped 1922
1878	Tamar	-	-	-	Ex-troopship used as Receiving Ship HK 1878; scuttled HK 1941
1882	Encounter	1970	16x64pdr	13	Wooden screw corvette built 1873; she and her sister ships were the fastest and most economical wooden cruising ships in service; involved in Battle of the Muddy Flats, Shanghai, 1882; sold 1888
1885	Glenogle	3749	-	15	McGregor, Gow & Co. fast cargo liner built 1882 chartered by the British Government as an armed merchant cruiser; present with the British Fleet at the annexation of Port Hamilton, Korea; sold to Burmese buyers 1904
1886	Leander	4300	10x6	16	2nd Class cruiser, built 1885; China 1886; Chatham 1896; Pacific 1897; Destroyer Depot ship 1902; Mediterranean 1904; Atlantic 1905; Norway 1906; Devonport 1907; Grand Fleet 1914; sold 1920
1888	Porpoise	1770	6x6, 3x14TT	16	Torpedo cruiser built 1888; China 1888; Australia 1897; refit Sheerness 1902; E Indies 1903; sold at Bombay 1905
1889	Imperieuse	8500	4x9, 10x6	17	Armoured cruiser built 1886; reserve, refit and removal of masts etc. 1886; Queen's Golden Jubilee Review 1887; re serve 1887; Flagship China 1889; refit 1894; Flagship Pacific 1896; refit Chatham 1899; depot ship for torpedo boats; Port land as HMS Sapphire II 1905; sold 1913
1890	Mercury	3730	13x5	17	Despatch vessel, built 1879; Portsmouth reserve 1879; China 1890; Portsmouth reserve 1895; navigation school ship 1903; submarine depot ship Portsmouth 1906; hulked at Chatham for service at Rosyth and renamed HMS Columbine; sold 1919
1891	Archer	1770	6x6, 3x14TT	16	Torpedo cruiser, built 1888; sold 1905
1891	Caroline	1420	14x5	13	Composite screw corvette built 1885; sold 1929
1891	Hyacinth	1420	14x5	13	Composite screw corvette built 1883; sold 1902
1891	Severn	4050	2x8,10x6	18	2nd class cruiser, built 1888; China 1889; Chatham reserve 1895; sold 1905
1892	TB 8, 9, 10, 11	28	-	20	Torpedo boats built 1878; scrapped HK c1900
1893	Undaunted	5600	2x9, 10x6	18	Armoured cruiser, built 1889; Devonport 1889; Med 1890; China 1893; Devonport 1901; sold 1907
1894	Edgar	7350	2x9, 10x6	19	1st Class protected cruiser built 1894; China 1894; Trooping 1898; Devonport trooping 1898; Devonport 1901; N America & W Indies 1905; trooping 1907; 4th Division 1909; 10th CS Northern patrol 1914; rebuilt with anti-mine bulges 1915; Dardanelles 1915; Aegean & Bulgarian coast 1917; Gibraltar 1918; sold 1920
1894	Centurion	10500	4x10, 10x4.7	18	2nd Class battleship built 1894; Flagship China, Relief of Legation Quarter, Peking; Capt. Jellicoe was her Flag Captain and was given command of the RN Landing Contingent of about 1000 men, with another 1000 provided by warships of the French, Italian, Russian, American, Japanese, German and Austro-Hungarian Navies; Jellicoe, who would command the RN Grand Fleet in WWI, was very seriously wounded; during this operation 4 Chinese destroyers, recently built in Germany were captured by an RN party under Roger Keyes, also later to become an Admiral, 1894; see Fame, 1996; reconstructed replacing the 10x4.7 guns with 10x6 guns and removing 5 of the 7x18 torpedo tubes 1901; China 1903; Home 1906; scrapped 1910
1895	Grafton	7350	2x9, 10x6	19	1st Class protected cruiser built 1894; Flagship China 1895; Chatham 1899; Pacific 1902; Portsmouth 1905; 10th CS North ern patrol 1914; rebuilt with anti-mine bulges 1915; Med 1916; Red Sea 1917; Aegean 1918; Black Sea 1919; sold 1920
1895	Immortalite	5600	2x9, 10x6	18	Armoured cruiser built 1889; Channel 1890; Chatham 1894; China 1895; Sheerness 1899; sold 1905
1895	Narcissus	5600	2x9, 10x6	18	Armoured cruiser built 1889; Channel 1892; Portsmouth 1895; China 1895; Portsmouth 1901; sold 1906
1895	Pique	3400	2x6, 6x4.7	20	2nd Class cruiser built 1890; Devonport 1892; China 1895; Devonport 1898; China 1900; Sheerness 1904; sold 1911

During the 1890s, Gibraltar, Hawke, Royal Arthur (ex-Centaur), St George & Theseus, 1st Class protected cruisers, built 1893-6, served on the China station.

DATE	NAME	TONS	ARMAMENT	SP	OUTLINE OF SERVICE HISTORY
1896	Fame	320	1x3, 2x18TT	30	Destroyer built 1896; China 1896; relief of Legation Quarter, Peking 1900; during this operation, she and Whiting captured 4 Chinese destroyers one of each of which were subsequently allocated to the Royal Navy and to the navies of France, Germany and Russia 1900; scrapped HK 1921
1896	Whiting	390	1x3, 2x18TT	30	Destroyer built 1897; see Fame, 1896; scrapped HK 1919
1897	Kinsha	616	2x3	14	River gunboat built 1897; sold by 1929
1897	Woodcock, Woodlark	150	2x6	13	River gunboats built 1897; sold by 1929
1897	Nightingale Sandpiper, Snipe	85	2x6	9	River gunboats built 1897; sold by 1929
1897	Robin	85	2x6	9	River gunboat built 1897; see Cicala, 1924; sold c1932
1898	Bonaventure	4360	2x6, 8x4.7	19	2nd Class cruiser built 1894; Flagship E Indies 1894; refit 1897; China 1998; grounded on E coast of Korea and repaired at HK 1899; refit 1901; Pacific 1903; submarine

DATE	NAME	TONS	ARMAMENT	SP	OUTLINE OF SERVICE HISTORY
1898	*Bonaventure* cont.				depot ship 1906; escorted *HM Submarines C36, C37& C38*, bound for HK, as far as Malta 1911; sold 1920
1898	*Hermione*	4360	2x6, 8x4.7	19	2nd Class cruiser built 1896; Channel 1896; China 1898; refit 1901; Med 1902; Portsmouth 1904; Cape Squadron (grounded off Zanzibar 1914) 1907; depot ship for patrol vessels, Southampton (burnt out 1916 but remained in partial service) 1914; became training ship *Warspite* on Thames 1922; sold 1940
1898	*Victorious*	14500	4x12, 12x6	17	1st Class battleship built 1896; China 1896; Med 1900; Guardship 1914; disarmed to provide 12 inch guns for monitors and became depot ship 1915; sold 1920-3
1898	*Barfleur*	10500	4x10, 10x4.7	18	2nd class battleship built 1894; Med 1895; China 1898; sold 1910
1898	*Powerful*	14200	2x9.2, 126	22	1st class protected cruiser built 1897; China 1898; refit 1902; Flagship Australia 1905; training ship 1913; renamed *HMS Impregnable* 1919; sold 1929
1899	*Orlando*	5600	2x9.2, 10x6	18	Armoured cruiser built 1889; Flagship Australia 1888; Portsmouth 1898; China 1899; Portsmouth 1903; sold 1905
1899	*Aurora*	5600	2x9.2, 10x6	18	Armoured cruiser built 1889; Channel 1890; Devonport 1892; China 1899; relief of Legation Quarter, Peking, 1900; see *Fame*, 1894; refit 1902; Devonport 1904; sold 1907
1899	*Terrible*	14200	2x9.2, 12x6	22	1st Class protected cruiser built 1898; Cape of Good Hope 1899; Refit 1902; China 1899; Portsmouth Reserve 1903; Flagship, Australia 1905; escorted *Renown* on Prince and Princess of Wales' cruise to India 1905; trooping to China 1906; 4th Division, Portsmouth 1907; Pembroke Reserve 1913; trooping to Dardanelles 1915; accomodation ship Portsmouth as part of *HMS Fisguard* 1916; sold 1932
1899	*Endymion*	7350	2x9.2, 10x6	20	1st Class protected cruiser built 1894; Channel 1894; Chatham 1897; China 1899; relief of Legation Quarter, 1900; refit 1902; Channel 1904; tender to *Wildfire* as gunnery training ship, Sheerness 1905; 3rd Fleet Portsmouth 1912; Flagship Training Sqn, Queenstown 1913; 10th CS, Northern patrol 1914; rebuilt with mine bulges 1915; Dardanelles 1915; Mediterranean 1916; Aegean 1918; Nore 1919; sold 1920
1899	*Glory*	12950	4x12, 12x6	18	1st Class battleship built 1900; China 1899; N Atlantic 1914; Med 1915; N Russia 1916; Depot ship, renamed *HMS Crescent* 1919; sold 1920
1900	*Argonaut*	11000	16x6, 14x3	21	1st Class protected cruiser built 1900; China 1900; Chatham 1904; nucleus crew 1906; Portsmouth 1909; 7th CS 1912; 9th CS mid-Atlantic 1914; Hospital ship Portsmouth 1915; sold *1920*
1900	*Goliath*	12950	4x12, 12x6	18	1st class battleship built 1900; China 1900; sunk by torpedo from *Turkish* TB Muavenet in the Eastern Mediterranean in 1915
1900	*Ocean*	12950	4x12,12x6	18	1st class battleship built 1900; China 1900; sunk by mine
1901	*Taku*	305	6x3, 3x18TT	32	Destroyer captured from Chinese; see *Fame*; sold; 1916
1901	*Blenheim*	9150	2x9.2, 10x6	22	1st Class protected cruiser built 1894; Chatham 1891; Channel 1894; China 1901; destroyer depot ship 1905; sold 1926
1901	*Cressy*	12000	2x9.2, 12x6	21	1st Class armoured cruiser built 1901; China 1901; Portsmouth 1904; N America & W Indies 1907; Nore 1909; 6th CS 1912; 7th CS 1914; torpedoed by U-18 1914 in North Sea
1901	*Albion*	12950	4x12, 12x6	18	1st Class battleship built 1901; China 1901; E Africa campaign 1914; off German SW Africa 1914; Dardanelles 1915; North Sea 1916; Depot ship 1918; sold 1919
1901	*Midge*	576	-	-	Ex-gun vessel built 1867; became Hospital Ship at HK; sold 1907
1901	*Teal, Moorhen*	180	2x6	13	River gunboats built 1901; sold c1925
1902	*Vengeance*	12950	4x12, 12x6	18	1st Class battleship built 1902; China 1902; Cameroons campaign 1914; Dardanelles 1915; Med, E Africa & Indies 1915; Depot ship 1918; sold 1921
1902	*Amphitrite*	11000	16x6, 14x3	21	1st class protected cruiser built 1901; China 1902; Chatham 1902; 9th CS 1914; Portsmouth 1915; converted to minelayer 1916; Nore 1917; sold 1920
1903	*Arun*	5500	4x3, 2x18TT	26	Destroyer built 1903; sold 1920
1903	*Itchen*	5500	4x3, 2x18TT	26	Destroyer built 1903; torpedoed by U-boat in North Sea
1904	*Widgeon*	195	2x6	13	River gunboat built 1904; sold 1931
1904	*Sparrowhawk*	355	-	30	Destroyer, built 1897; wrecked in Yangtze river 1904
1905	*Phoenix*	1050	6x4	13	Steel crew sloop built 1896; capsized off HK 1906 during a typhoon
1906	*Kent*	9800	14x6, 10x3	23	Armoured cruiser built 1903; China 1906; refit 1913; sank *SMS Nurnburg* at Battle of Falkland Islands 1914; with *Glasgow*, sank *SMS Dresden* at Mas-a-fuera island 1915; Pacific 1915; Cape of Good Hope 1916; China 1918; Vladivostok 1919; sold in HK 1920
1906	*King Alfred*	14150	2x9.2, 16x6	23	1st Class armoured cruiser built 1903; Flagship China 1906; 6th CS Grand Fleet 1914; sold 1920
1906	*Monmouth*	9800	14x6, 10x3	23	Armoured cruiser built 1903; China 1906; 5th CS mid-Atlantic, sunk with all hands by gunfire of *SMS Scharnhorst & Gneisenau* at Battle of Coronel, 1914
1907	*Bedford*	9800	14x6, 10x3	23	Armoured cruiser built 1903; China, wrecked on Cheduba island, 1910; wreck sold 1910
1911	*Hart*	2750		25	Destroyer built 1896; scrapped HK 1911
1911	*C36, 37, 38*	290	-	14	Submarines built 1910; escorted as far as Malta by *Bonaventure* (see 1898); sold in China 1919
1912	*Hampshire*	10850	4x7.5, 6x6	22	1st Class armoured cruiser built 1905; sank German auxiliary ship *SS Elspeth* in China Sea 1914; took part, with *Minotaur, Yarmouth, Empress of Russia & Empress of Asia*, HIJMS *Ibuki*, *Tokiwa, Yakumo, Chikuma & Yahagi*, Russian cruisers *Askold & Zhemchug*, and French cruiser *D'Iberville* in the hunt for *SMS Emden*, 1914; *Emden* missed at Simaloer island, Dutch East Indies, by a mere 20 miles and again in the Bay of Bengal, 1914; Northern patrols 1915; Battle of Jutland 1916; mined off Orkneys with Lord Kitchener aboard, 1916
1913	*Janus*	275	-	27	Destroyer built 1895; scrapped HK 1913
1913	*Hercules*	170	-	-	War Department vessel built 1898
1913	*Jubilee*	60	-	-	War Department vessel built 1887
1913	*Omphale*	140	-	-	War Department vessel built 1905
1913	*Tommy Atkins*	120	-	-	War Department vessel built 1898

DATE	NAME	TONS	ARMAMENT	SP	OUTLINE OF SERVICE HISTORY
1914	Triumph	11985	4x10, 14x7.5	20	Ex-Chilean *Libertad* 2nd Class Battleship; built 1904; demilitarised in HK 1914; hastily re-commissioned with crews from gunboat flotilla and 100 volunteers from the Duke of Cornwall's Light Infantry from the HK garrison 1914; took part with the Japanese Navy in the blockade and siege of the German base at Tsingtao; torpedoed by *U-21* 1915 off the Dardanelles
1914	Swiftsure	11985	4x10, 14x7.5	20	Ex-Chilean *Consticion* 2nd class Battleship, built 1904; sold 1920
1914	Astraea	4360	2x6, 8x4.7	19	2nd class cruiser built 1895; sold 1920
1914	Flora	4360	2x6, 8x4.7	19	2nd class cruiser built 1893; sold 1922
1914	Monmouth	9800	14x6, 10x3	23	1st class armoured cruiser built 1903; sunk by gunfire of *Scharnhorst* & *Gneisenau* at Battle of Coronel, 1914
1914	Minotaur	14600	4x9.2, 10x7.5	23	1st class armoured cruiser built 1908; China 1914; with *Newcastle* destroyed the German radio station at Yap 1914; took part in the hunt for *SMS Emden*, see *Hampshire* 1914; North Sea & 2nd CS 1915; Battle of Jutland 1916; Flagship 2nd CS 1918; sold 1920
1914	Newcastle	4800	2x6, 10x4	26	Light cruiser built 1910; China 1914; see *Minotaur* 1914; Pacific 1915; Med & Indian Ocean 1917; S Atlantic 1918; Med, E Indies & Adriatic 1919; SE coast of S America 1918; Nore Reserve 1919; sold 1921
1914	Yarmouth	5250	8x6, 1x3	25	Light cruiser built 1912; took part in the hunt for *SMS Emden*, see *Minotaur*, 1914; sank *Emden*'s auxiliary *SS Markomannia* off Simaloer island, Sumatra 1914; Grand Fleet 1915; Battle of Jutland 1916; 2nd CS Grand Fleet 1918; Flagship, Cape of Good Hope 1919; refit 1919; 7th LCS S America 1919; Nore Reserve 1920; Signal School, Portsmouth 1922; refit 1924; trooping 1925; Signal School, Portsmouth 1927; Flagship, Rear-Admiral, Submarines, Falmouth 1928; sold 1929
1914	Empress of Russia	-	-	-	Fitted out at HK as armed merchant cruiser, manned by RN personnel from gunboats, her own Chinese crew, volunteers from the shore, RM Guard from Wei-Hai-Wei, and personnel of the French Navys' gunboats in China. This crew was described by the Admiralty "as a miscellaneous and possibly unique crew, who throughout worked together in perfect - although occasionally vociferous - harmony; took part in the hunt for *SMS Emden*, see *Minotaur*, 1914
1914	Empress of Asia	-	-	-	Fitted out at HK as armed merchant cruiser, partly manned by RN personnel from gunboats plus 1 officer and 20 men from the Royal Artillery and 25 men from 40th Pathans; took part in the hunt for *SMS Emden*, see *Minotaur*, 1914
1914	Himalaya	-	-	-	Fitted out at HK as armed merchant cruiser
1914	TB 35, 36, 37, 38	63	-	18	Torpedo boats built 1886; *TB 37* towed *SS Tai On*, pirated in the Pearl River estuary and burnt out, over 250 people having lost their lives, to HK 1913; scrapped 1919
1914	Bramble	1650	-	17	Despatch vessel built 1885; scrapped Bombay 1920
1914	Cadmus, Clio	1070	6x4	13	Gunboats built 1903; scrapped HK c1921
1914	Thistle	701	2x4, 4x3	13	Gunboat built 1898; scrapped Bombay 1926

DATE	NAME	TONS	ARMAMENT	SP	OUTLINE OF SERVICE HISTORY
1914	Alacrity	701	2x4, 4x3	13	Gunboat built 1898; scrapped 1920s
1914	Britomart	701	2x4, 4x3	13	Gunboat built 1898; scrapped Bombay 1920
1914	Chelmer, Colne Jed, Kennet, Usk Welland, Ribble	5500	4x3, 2x18TT	26	Destroyers built 1904; Med. 1911; China 1913; scrapped c1920
1915	Rosario	980	-	13	Sloop built 1898; later Submarine Depot Ship; sold HK 1921
1917	Otter	355	-	-	Destroyer built 1900; HK 1914; scrapped 1917
1919	Cairo	4290	5x6, 2x3	29	Light cruiser built 1919; 5th LCS China 1919; 4th CS E Indies 1922; 8th CS N America & W Indies 1926; Med. 1928; converted to AA cruiser with 8x4 guns 1938; Channel 1939; Med, torpedoed by Italian submarine *Axum* off Bizerta and finally sunk by *HMS Pathfinder* 1942
1919	Carlisle	4290	5x6, 2x3	29	Light cruiser, ex-*HMS Cawnpore*, built 1918; 5th LCS China 1919; 6th CS Africa 1929; converted to AA cruiser with 8x4 guns 1939; Home 1940; Med 1941-43; bombed by Italian air craft and declared constructive total loss 1943; scrapped in 1949
1919	Colombo	4290	5x6, 2x3	29	Light cruiser built 1919; 5th LCS China 1919; 4th LCS E Indies 1921; 8th CS N America & W Indies 1926; 3rd CS 1932; 4th CS E Indies 1933; Gibraltar 1939-43; converted to AA cruiser with 8x4 guns 1942; scrapped 1948
1919	Hawkins	9800	7x7.5, 5x4	30	Cruiser built 1920; Shanghai & South Atlantic 1940; E Indies 1941; Eastern Fleet 1942; Home 1944; scrapped 1947
1920	Curlew	4290	5x6, 2x3	29	Light cruiser built 1917; 5th LCS Harwich 1917; Baltic 1919; 5th LCS China 1920; Empire cruise 1922; 5th CS China 1927; converted to AA cruiser with 10x4 guns 1935; Home Fleet, bombed and sunk by Luftwaffe off Norway 1940
1920	Cicala	625	2x6, 1x3	14	River gunboat built 1915; served on the Divina River, North Russia 1919-20; with *HMS Robin* and 4 Chinese gunboats, under a Chinese Admiral, she was involved in an abortive operation against alleged pirates in the Konmoon area 1924; sunk by Japanese aircraft HK 1941
1920	Moth	625	2x6, 1x3	14	River gunboat built 1915; sunk by Japanese aircraft HK 1941
1920	Hydrangea	1250	2x4.7	17	Fleetsweeping sloop built 1916; sold HK for commercial use 1920; *SS Hydrangea* was attacked by pirates masquerading as saloon and deck passengers; in 1923, she was taken into Bias Bay and looted in her own boats which took the pirates ashore 1923
1920	Wanderer	1325	4x4.7	34	Destroyer built 1919; sank 5 U-boats between 1941-4; scrapped 1946
1920	Wolverine	1325	4x4.7	34	Destroyer built 1920; sank 3 U-boats between 1941-2; scrapped 1945
1921	Durban	4850	6x6, 3x4	29	Light cruiser built 1921; 5th CS China 1921; 3rd CS Med 1933; China 1939; bombed during evacuation of Singapore 1942; Eastern Fleet 1942; Home, scuttled as breakwater off Normandy beaches 1944
1922	Marazion	820	1x4, 1x3	16	Minesweeper built 1919; see *Hermes*, 1927; sold HK 1933
1922	Diomede	4850	6x6, 3x4	29	Light cruiser built 1922; 5th CS China 1922; New Zealand 1925; Med 1936; America & W Indies 1939; S Atlantic 1942; scrapped 1946
1922	L4	790	1x3, 4x21TT	17	Submarine built 1918; fired at pirated *SS Irene* and set her on

DATE	NAME	TONS	ARMAMENT	SP	OUTLINE OF SERVICE HISTORY
1922	L4 cont.				fire causing passengers and crew to jump overboard. *L4*'s crew rescued 224 by jumping into the sea 1927; sold 1934
1922	L5	790	1x3, 4x21TT	17	Submarine built 1918; with *Magnolia* and *Stormcloud* picked up 12 more survivors from *SS Irene* 1927; sold 1935
1922	L6, L7, L8	790	1x3, 4x21TT	17	Submarines built 1918; sold 1930
1922	L9	790	1x3, 4x21TT	17	Submarine built 1918; foundered in typhoon in HK 1923; later raised and sold
1923	Merlin	1070	-	13	Sloop built 1901; converted to surveying ship; sold HK 1923
1925	Petersfield	710	1x4	16	Minesweeper converted to CinC's yacht; lost 1932
1925	Vindictive	9770	5x7.5, 5x4	30	Cruiser ex-*HMS Cavendish*, completed as a light aircraft carrier, converted back to cruiser; with, *Hermes* and *Despatch* searched for missing lifeboats from the pirated and burning *SS Sunning* 1926; training ship 1936; repair ship 1939; S Atlantic 1940; Med 1943; Home 1945; scrapped 1946
1925	Concord	4165	5x6, 1x3	29	Light cruiser built 1916; 5th LCS Harwich 1916; 3rd LCS Med 1919; China 1925; sold 1935
1926	Bluebell	1250	2x4	15	*Flower* class minesweeping sloop built 1915; went to the assistance of the pirated *SS Sunning*; she took onboard the people rescued by *SS Ravensfjell*, also one lifeboat with escaping pirates
1926	Cornwall	9750	8x8, 4x4	31	Cruiser built 1928; 5th CS 1926; 2nd CS Home 1938; 5th CS China 1939; S Atlantic 1940; E Indies, sunk by Japanese aircraft W of Ceylon 1942
1926	Caradoc	4180	5x6, 2x3	29	Light cruiser built 1917; 6th LCS Grand Fleet 1917; Baltic 1918; 3rd LCS Med 1919; China 1926; 8th CS N America & W Indies 1928; 5th CS China 1930; Channel 1939; America & W Indies 1939; Eastern Fleet 1942; South Atlantic 1943; Eastern Fleet 1944; scrapped 1946
1926	Despatch	4650	6x6, 2x3	28	Light cruiser built 1919; see *Vindictive*, 1925; America & W Indies 1939; S Atlantic 1942; Home 1944; scrapped 1946
1920s	Eagle	22600	9x6, 4x4	24	Originally ordered by the Chilean Navy as a battleship, she was bought incomplete on the stocks, by the RN and completed as an aircraft carrier; alternated stationing at HK with *Hermes* between the wars; E Indies 1939; Med 1940; S Atlantic 1941; Force 'H' 1942; torpedoed in Mediterranean 1942
1926	Hermes	10850	6x5.5, 3x4	25	First aircraft carrier originally designed as such; with *Frobisher, Delhi, Foxglove & Marazion*, following the pirating of *SS Hopsang*, made a punitive expedition against pirate lairs in Bias Bay 1927; Home 1939; E Indies 1939; Eastern Fleet 1942; sunk by Japanese aircraft off Ceylon 1942
1927	Foxglove	1200	2x4	16	*Flower* class minesweeping sloop built 1915; with *Hermes, Frobisher, Delhi & Marazion*, following the pirating of *SS Hopsang*, made a punitive expedition against pirate lairs in Bias Bay 1927
1927	Cator	4320	4x6, 2x3	28	Light cruiser built 1915; Grand Fleet, Battle of Jutland 1916; Black Sea 1919; Irish patrols 1922; trooping to China 1927; sold 1935
1927	Dauntless	4850	6x6, 3x4	29	Light cruiser built 1918; Baltic operations 1919; Empire cruise 1923; China 1927; 8th CS N America & W Indies 1928; 3rd CS Med 1932; 9th CS S Atlantic 1939; China 1939; Eastern
1927	Dauntless cont.				Fleet 1942; scrapped 1946
1927	Dragon	4850	6x6, 3x4	29	Light cruiser built 1918; Baltic operations 1919; Empire cruise 1923; China 1927; 8th CS N America & W Indies 1930; Home, Med. & W Indies 1ndies, S Atlantic 1940; Eastern Fleet 1942; Home, manned by Polish Navy, 1943; badly damaged by a *Marder* 1944, and scuttled as a breakwater off Normandy beaches
1927	Bruce	1800	5x4.7, 6x21TT	36	Built 1919, leader of 8th Destroyer Flotilla China 1927; sunk as a target 1939
1927	Delhi	4650	6x6, 12x21TT	28	Light Cruiser built 1919; Baltic operations 1919; Flagship 1st LCS Atlantic 1919; Empire cruise 1919; 1st CS Mediterranean 1925; China 1927; see *Hermes*, 1927 for Bias Bay landings; refit 1928; 8th CS America & WI; 3rd CS Med 1932; Devonport reserve 1938; 12th/11th CS Home 1939; Med. 1940; Atlantic 1941; rearmed NY Navy Yard 1941; Home 1942; Med 1943; scrapped 1948
1927	Frobisher	9750	7x7.5, 6x21TT	31	Cruiser built 1924; 1st LCS Med. 1924; China 1927; see *Hermes*, 1927; Flagship 1st CS Med 1928; 2nd CS Atlantic 1929; reserve 1930; Training Ship 1932; reserve 1937; rearmed 1939; 4th CS Eastern Fleet 1942; 1st CS Home Fleet, damaged by torpedo 1944; Training ship 1945; scrapped 1949
1927	Stronghold	905	3x4, 4x21TT	36	Destroyer built 1919; escaped HK to Singapore; 1941; sunk in Batle of Java Sea 1942
1927	Tenedos	905	3x4, 4x21TT	36	Destroyer built 1919; escaped HK 1941; joined Force Z with *Prince of Wales* and *Repulse* at Singapore 1941; bombed and sunk at Colombo 1942
1927	Thanet	905	3x4, 4x21TT	36	Destroyer built 1919; escaped to Singapore 1941; sunk in action with Japanese off Malaya 1942
1927	Thracian	905	3x4, 4x21TT	36	Destroyer built 1922; Scuttled HK 1941; salved by Japanese and converted to patrol boat; recovered 1945 and scrapped 1946
1927	Stormcloud	1075	3x4, 4x21TT	36	S class destroyer built 1919; with *Magnolia & L5* picked up survivors of pirated *SS Irene* 1927; sold 1933
1927	Sterling	1075	3x4, 4x21TT	36	S class destroyer built 1919; following the pirating and burning of *SS Haiching*, went alongside to try to fight the fire and tow *Haiching* to HK 1929; sold 1932
1927	Sirdar	1075	3x4, 4x21TT	36	S class destroyer built 1918; Sirdar took the rescued passengers off *Sterling* so that the latter could tow *SS Haiching* to HK; sold 1933
1927	Tern	262	2x3	14	River gunboat built 1927; scuttled at HK 1941
1927	Gannet	310	2x3	16	River gunboat built 1927; presented to China and renamed *Ying Shan* (British Mountain) 1942
1927	Petrel	310	2x3	16	River gunboat built 1927; sunk in action with Japanese coast defence ship, ex-armoured cruiser, *HIJMS Idzumo,* Shanghai 1941
1928	Kent	9850	8x8, 8x4	31	Cruiser built 1928; 5th CS China 1928; E Indies 1939; Home 1940; scrapped 1948
1928	Suffolk	9800	8x8, 8x4	31	Cruiser built 1926; 5th CS China 1928; Home 1939; Eastern Fleet 1943; scrapped 1948
1928	Berwick	9750	8x8, 8x4	31	Cruiser built 1928; 5th CS China 1928; Home, 1939; forced German blockade runners *SSs Wolfsburg & Uruguay* to scuttle

DATE	NAME	TONS	ARMAMENT	SP	OUTLINE OF SERVICE HISTORY
1928	*Berwick* cont.				themselves 1940; Med 1940; Force 'H' 1940; Home Fleet 1941; scrapped 1948
1928	*Cumberland*	9750	8x8, 8x4	31	Cruiser built 1928; 5th CS China 1928; Shanghai during Japanese troubles 1937; 2nd CS Home 1939; S Atlantic 1939; Home 1941; Eastern Fleet 1944; 5th CS E Indies 1945; converted to trials cruiser 1949; scrapped 1959
1928	*Cleopatra*	4219	4x6, 2x3	28	Light cruiser built 1915; 5th LCS Harwich; rammed and sank German destroyer *G-194*, 1916; mined off Dutch coast 1916; 7th LCS Grand Fleet 1918; 2nd LCS Baltic 1919; trooping to China 1928-29; sold 1931
1928	*Constance*	4320	4x6, 2x3	28	Light cruiser built 1916; 4th LCS (Battle of Jutland 1916) 1916; 8th LCS N America & W Indies 1919; 5th CS China 1918; sold 1936
1929	*Devonshire*	9750	8x8, 4x4	32	Cruiser built 1929; 5th CS China 1st CS Med 1933; 1st CS Home 1939; Eastern Fleet 1942; 1st CS 1944; scrapped 1954
1929	*Cambrian*	4320	4x6, 2x3	28	Light cruiser built 1916; 4th LCS Grand Fleet 1916; 8th LCS N America & W Indies 1919; 2nd LCS Atlantic 1926; trooping to China 1929; sold 1934
1930	*Canterbury*	4320	4x6, 2x3	28	Light cruiser built 1916; Battle of Jutland 1916; 5th LCS Harwich 1916; Aegean and Black Sea 1918; trooping to China 1930; sold 1934
1931	*Falcon*	372	1x3.7	15	River gunboat built 1931; presented to China and renamed *Ying Teh* (British Virtue)
1931	Unknown (x4)	1120	4x4.7	34	Modified *W* Class destroyer built 1918; HK as 8th Destroyer Flotilla 1931
1932	*Comet, Crescent Crusader, Cygnet*	1375	4x4.7	36	Destroyers built 1932; HK 8th Destroyer Flotilla 1932 transferred to Canadian Navy, 1937
c1932	*Odin*	1311	1x4, 8x21TT	17	Submarine built 1928; missing 1940
c1932	*Otus*	1311	1x4, 8x21TT	17	Submarine built 1928; scrapped post-war
c1932	*Olympus*	1311	1x4, 8x21TT	17	Submarine built 1929; mined off Malta 1942
c1932	*Orpheus*	1311	1x4, 8x21TT	17	Submarine built 1929; missing 1940
c1932	*Osiris*	1311	1x4, 8x21TT	17	Submarine built 1928; scrapped post-war
c1932	*Oswald*	1311	1x4, 8x21TT	17	Submarine built 1928; sunk by Italian destroyer *Ugolino Vivaldi* in Ionian Sea 1940
c1932	*Oberon*	1311	1x4, 8x21TT	17	Submarine built 1926; scrapped post-war
c1932	*Otway*	1311	1x4, 8x21TT	17	Submarine built for Australia 1926; transferred to RN 1931; scrapped post-war
c1932	*Oxley*	1311	1x4, 8x21TT	17	Submarine built 1928; lost by explosion 1939
1933	*Sandpiper*	185	1x3.7	11	River gunboat built 1933; presented to China and renamed *Ying Hao* (British Hero) 1942
1934	*Defender*	1375	4x4.7	34	Destroyer built 1932; HK as 32nd Destroyer Flotilla 1934; sunk by bombs Sidi Barrani 1941
1934	*Diamond*	1375	4x4.7	34	Destroyer built 1932; HK as 32nd Destroyer Flotilla 1934; sunk by enemy aircraft in Gulf of Nauplia 1941
1934	*Daring*	1375	4x4.7	34	Destroyer built 1932; HK as 32nd Destroyer Flotilla 1934; torpedoed by U-boat in North Sea 1940
1934	*Decoy*	1375	4x4.7	34	Destroyer built 1932; HK as 32nd Destroyer Flotilla 1934; transferred to Canadian Navy 1943
1934	*Dainty*	1375	4x4.7	34	Destroyer built 1932; HK as 32nd Destroyer Flotilla 1934; sank 2 U-boats 1940, sunk by aircraft off Tobruk
1934	*Delight*	1375	4x4.7	34	Destroyer built 1932; HK as 32nd Destroyer Flotilla 1934;

DATE	NAME	TONS	ARMAMENT	SP	OUTLINE OF SERVICE HISTORY
1934	*Delight* cont...				sunk by enemy aircraft off Portland 1940
1934	*Diana*	1375	4x4.7	34	Destroyer built 1932; HK as 32nd Destroyer Flotilla 1934; transferred to Canadian Navy 1940
1934	*Duchess*	1375	4x4.7	34	Destroyer built 1932; HK as 32nd Destroyer Flotilla 1934; sunk in collision in North Channel 1939
1934	*Robin*	226	1x3.7	13	River gunboat built 1934; scuttled HK 1941
1934	*Capetown*	4290	5x6, 2x3	29	Light cruiser built 1922; 8th LCS N America & W Indies 1922; 5th CS China 1934; guardship at Nanking and Hankow since before the Sino-Japanese Incident 1937 began; Med 1939; E Indies 1941; Eastern Fleet 1942; Home 1944; scrapped 1946
1935	*Dorsetshire*	9750	8x8, 4x4	32	Cruiser built 1930; Home 1930; Flagship 6th CS Africa 1933; 5th LCS China 1935; S Atlantic 1940; torpedoed *Bismarck* 1941; Eastern Fleet, sunk by Japanese aircraft W of Ceylon 1942
1937	*Birmingham*	9100	12x6, 8x4	32	Cruiser built 1937; Flagship 5th CS China 1937; 18th CS Home 1940; Flagship S America 1941; 4th CS Eastern Fleet 1942; 10th CS Home 1945; 4th CS E Indies 1947; 5th CS Far East 1952; Home 1957; Med 1959; scrapped 1960
1937	*Danae*	4850	6x6, 3x4	29	Light cruiser built 1918; Baltic operations 1919; Empire Cruise 1923; 1st CS Med 1925; 8th CS N America & W Indies 1930; China 1939, Eastern Fleet 1942; Home, transferred to Polish Navy as *PS Conrad* 1944
1937	*Scorpion*	700	2x4	17	River gunboat built 1937; scuttled at Singapore 1941
1938	*MTB 07, 08, 09, 10, 11, 12, 26, 27*	18	2x18TT	35	Motor Torpedo Boats built 1937; sunk in HK 1942; it is believed 2 of the MTBs may have escaped to China
1938	*Cardiff*	4290	5x6, 2x3	29	Ex-*HMS Caprice* light cruiser built 1917; 6th LCS Grand Fleet 1917; led German High Seas Fleet to surrender 1918; Baltic 1918; 3rd LCS Med 1919; 6th CS Africa; 5th CS China 1938; Home 1939; scrapped 1946
1938	*Liverpool*	9400	12x6, 8x4	32	Cruiser built 1938; 5th CS China 1938; Red Sea and Med 1942; 1st CS Med 1945; scrapped 1952
1939	*Redstart*	498	-	10	Coastal minelayer built 1939; China 1939; Lost HK 1941
1941	*Cornflower*	1250	2x4.7	17	Minesweeping sloop built 1916; RNVR drillship in HK between the Wars; lost 1941

At the end of the Second World War many ships from the British Pacific Fleet visited Hong Kong. In particular:

DATE	NAME	TONS	ARMAMENT	SP	OUTLINE OF SERVICE HISTORY
1945	*Indomitable*	23000	16x4.5, 72pl	32	Aircraft Carrier built 1940; Home 1941; Eastern Fleet 1942; Home 1942; Force 'H' 1943; Eastern Fleet 1944; British Pacific Fleet, 1945; task force to enter HK after launching the last air strikes of the War by her Hellcats of 839 Sqn and 844 Sqn & Avengers of 857 Sqn against Japanese suicide craft hidden among the islands around HK 1945; scrapped 1955
1945	*Venerable*	13190	48pl	25	Aircraft carrier built 1944; Pacific Fleet; task force to enter HK after launching, with *Indomitable*, the final air strikes of the War with her Corsairs of 850 Sqn and Barracudas of 812 Sqn against Japanese suicide craft; her officers and men rehabilitated the premises of the Royal Hong Kong Yacht which was re-opened 17th Sep 45 with a 4-dinghy race, a 21-gun salute, a flypast of Corsairs and a firework and searchlight

DATE	NAME	TONS	ARMAMENT	SP	OUTLINE OF SERVICE HISTORY
1945	Venerable cont...				display; evacuated 354 British and Australian ex-POWs from Korea to Manila 1945; transferred to Royal Netherlands Navy as *Karel Doorman* 1948; sold to Argentina as *Veinticinco De Mayo* (*25th May*) 1968; took no part in Falklands War 1982; virtually gutted and awaiting decision on further refit 1997
1945	Vengeance	13190	48pl	25	Ex-*HMS Brave*, aircraft carrier built 1945; Pacific Fleet, part of Task Force to enter HK 1945; fitted for expermental work in Arctic 1948; Flagship, 3rd Aircraft Carrier Squadron 1950; loaned to Australian Navy 1953; sold to Brazilian Navy as *Minas Gerias* 1956; reconstructed at Rotterdam 1957; refit 1981; modernised 1991
1945	Anson	36830	10x14, 16x5.25	27	Ex-*HMS Jellicoe* battleship built 1942; Home 1942; Pacific Fleet, part of Task Force to enter HK 1945; Guardship Tokyo 1945; Australia 1946; Training Squadron 1948; reserve 1950; scrapped 1957
1945	Swiftsure	8800	9x6, 10x4	31	Cruiser built 1944; 10th CS Home 1944; Flagship 4th CS Pacific Fleet; led fleet into HK 1945; Japanese surrender of HK signed aboard 1945; Flagship 4th CS E Indies 1946; Flagship 2nd CS Home 1950; Home 1953; badly damaged in collision with *HMS Diamond* 1953; scrapped 1962
1945	Bermuda	8525	9x6, 8x4	32	Cruiser built 1942; 10th CS Home 1942; Pacific Fleet 1945; Flagship 5th CS Far East 1946; Flagship CinC S Atlantic 1950; Med 1953; Home Fleet 1955; scrapped 1965
1945	Maidstone	9000	8x4.5	17	Submarine Depot ship built 1938
1945	Selene, Supreme Sidon, Spearhead Solent, Sea Scout Sleuth, Scotsman	715	1x3, 6x21 TT	14	Submarines built 1944
1945	Smiter	11420	2x4	17	Ex-*USS Vermillion* escort aircraft carrier built 1945; Med 1945; East Indies Fleet 1945; brought 3rd Commando Brigade (2 Royal Marine & 2 Army Commandos) and a sqn of Spitfires to HK 1945; returned USN 1946; became *SS Artillero* 1948; became *SS President Garcia* 1965; wrecked off Guernsey 1967
1945	Adamant	12500	8x4.5	17	Submarine depot ship built 1942; she was mother ship to 4th Submarine Flotilla in HK; helped rehabilitate Royal Hong Kong Yacht Club 1945;
1945	Gambia	8525	12x6, 8x4	32	Cruiser built 1942; Eastern Fleet 1942; E Indies and Eastern Fleet 1943; Pacific Fleet 1945; Tokyo Bay surrender 1945; New Zealand 1945; 5th CS Far East 1946; Med. 1950; E Indies 1951; Med 1952; E Indies 1955; Home/Med. 1958; S Atlantic and Far East 1959; Home 1960; scrapped 1968
1945	Newfoundland	8875	9x6, 8x4	31	Cruiser built 1943; 10th CS Home 1943; Flagship 15th CS Med 1943; Pacific Fleet 1945; Flagship 5th CS Far East 1946; sold to Peruvian Navy and renamed *Almirante Grau* 1959
1945	Alert	1600	2x4	19	Ex-*HMS Dundrum Bay*, ex-*HMS Loch Scamadale*, frigate completed as CinC's yacht for Far East 1945

The greater part of the British Pacific Fleet's Fleet Train came to Hong Kong to set about the task of rehabilitating the Colony. These included the following ships:-

Lothian, Glenearn, Maidstone, Bonaventure, Aorangi, Lancashire, Artifex, Resource, Berry Head, Flamborough Head, Dullisk

Cove, Assistance, Diligence, Kelantan, Arbutus, Brown Ranger, Vacport, Seven Sisters, Bacchus, Tjittjalengka, Maunganui, Oxfordshire, Gerusalemme, Hermelin, Empire Josephine and Empire Sam (later RHKP), *Cockade, City of Dieppe, Fort Wrangell, Glenartney, Cossack, Rame Head, Serbol*

The following ships were among those serving in the Far East in the immediate post-war years:

DATE	NAME	TONS	ARMAMENT	SP	OUTLINE OF SERVICE HISTORY
1946	Belfast	10260	12x6, 12x4	32	Cruiser built 1939; 2nd CS/18th CS Home Fleet 1939; Flagship 10th CS Home Fleet 1942; British Pacific Fleet 1945; 5th CS Far East 1948; Korean War 1951; Flagship 5th CS & FO 2 i/c Far East 1952; Flagship Home Flotillas 1962; museum ship in Pool of London 1971
1946	Aire	1370	2x4	19	Twin screw corvette built 1943; renamed *HMS Tamar* as Base Ship, HK 1946; renamed *HMS Aire* 1946; stranded on Bombay Shoal, near Singapore and was a total loss; crew saved by *HMS Bonaventure*
1947	London	9.750	8x8, 4x4	32	Cruiser built 1929; 1st CS Med 1929; Home and South Atlantic 1941; Eastern Fleet 1944; 5th CS East Indies 1945; 5th CS Far East (badly damaged by Chinese gunfire while trying to rescue *Amethyst*) 1947; scrapped 1950
1947	Sussex	9750	8x8, 4x4	32	Cruiser built 1929; 1st CS Med 1929; South Atlantic 1939; East Indies and Home Fleet (bombed in dock and partially capsized at Greenock 1940); Eastern Fleet 1943; East Indies 1945; Flagship 5th CS Far East 1947; sold 1950
1949	Consort	1700	4x4.5, 4x21 TT	33	Destroyer built 1945; Yangtse incident 1949
1949	Concord	1710	4x4.5, 4x21 TT	33	Ex-*HMS Corso* destroyer built 1946; Yangtse incident 1949; fired upon by Chinese shore guns in Lema channel 1950;
1949	Jamaica	8525	12x6, 8x4	32	Cruiser built 1942; 10th CS Home 1942; 5th CS then 4th CS 1945; 5th CS Far East 1949; Home 1954; 1st CS Med 1954; Home 1957; scrapped 1962
1949	Morecombe Bay Cardigan Bay, Mounts Bay, St Bride's Bay	1600	4x4	19	Built 1949; Far East 1949; Korean War 1950;
1949	Mendip	1000	6x4	27	*Hunt* class frigate built 1940; loaned to China for 5 years and renamed *Lin Fu* 1948; returned to RN as *HMS Mendip* at HK 1949; transferred to Egyptian Navy 1949
1950	Loch Katrine	1435	1x4	19	Frigate built 1944; East Indies 1945; sold to RNZN as *Rotoiti* 1949; damaged in collision off HK 1950; modernised 1956; scrapped HK 1967
1950	Ceylon	8875	9x6, 8x4	31	Cruiser built 1943; 10th CS Home 1943; Eastern Fleet 1943; 5th CS East Indies 1945; Korea (embarked a battalion of the HK garrison for the Korean War) 1950; Flagship CinC East Indies 1952; Med (Suez Crisis) 1956; Flagship East Indies 1957; Home 1958; Med and Far East 1959; sold to Peruvian Navy
1950	Kenya	8525	12x6, 8x4	31	Cruiser built 1940; Home Fleet 194; Eastern Fleet 1943; 5th CS Eastern Fleet 1944; America & West Indies 1946; Flagship CinC Far East, Korean War 1950; Flagship CinC East Indies 1952; Home Fleet 1955; Flagship CinC America & West Indies 1956; Home Fleet 1956; scrapped 1962
1950	Unicorn	14750	8x4.5, 35pl	22	Aircraft maintenance carrier doubling as an operational

1950   *Unicorn* cont...

carrier built 1943; Home and Med 1943; Eastern Fleet 1944; British Fleet 1945; embarked a British battalion of the HK garrison for the Korean War 1950; scrapped 1959

With Singapore becoming the base for the Royal Navy's Far East Fleet, and the closure of the Dockyard in Hong Kong, ship visits, although still frequent, tended to be for R&R purposes. Visitors included:

Puma, Reliant, Tenby, Torquay, Blackpool, Salisbury, Albion, Eastbourne, Yarmouth, Plymouth, Tiger, Berwick, Rhyl, Hermes, Bulwark, Centaur, Whitby, Leopard, Eagle, Dido, Londonderry, Lowestoft, Euryalus, Arethusa, Lincoln, Cleopatra, Leopard, Defiance, Leander, Lynx, Jaguar, Ajax, Minerva, Danae, Andromeda, Nubian, Hermione, Achilles, Charybdis, Falmouth, Argonaut, Blake, Jupiter, Amazon, Diomede, Alacrity, Arrow, Naiad, Galatea, Rothesay, Aurora, Intrepid

Hong Kong remained a base for a number of small patrol craft, including Seaward Defence Motor Launches, motor minesweepers, Admiralty Motor Fishing Vessels and Landing Craft Assault Vessels.

DATE	NAME	TONS	ARMAMENT	SP	OUTLINE OF SERVICE HISTORY
1958	*Damersham* *Darsham* *Davenham* *Glentham* *Hovingham*	-	-	-	120th Minesweeping Sqn; Borneo patrols; transferred to Inshore Flotilla Singapore, 1967
1958	*Chichester*	2170	2x4.5	25	Aircraft Direction Frigate built 1958; Home/Far East 1958; Guardship HK 1974; scrapped 1981
1962	*Dufton* *Penston* *Lanton*				8th Minesweeping Sqn; Borneo patrols; transferred to inshore flotilla Singapore, 1967
1969	*Hubberston* *Sheraton* *Kirkliston* *Maxton* *Bossington*	360	2x40mm	15	Mine Hunters built c1956 6th Mine Counter-measure Sqn; scrapped 1980s
1971	*Beachampton* *Monkton* *Yarnton* *Wasperton* *Wolverton*	360	2x40mm	15	Ton class minesweepers built 1953; 6th Patrol Sqn HK 1971; disposed c1984
1984	*Swallow* *Swift*	690	1x3	25	Purpose built HK patrol craft built c1984; sold to Irish Navy 1988
1984	*Peacock* *Plover* *Starling*	690	1x3	25	Purpose built patrol craft built c1984; sold to Philippine Navy 1997

During the 1980s and 1990s, with the reduction in major Far East deployments, visiting British warships to Hong Kong proved few and far between, but included:

Britannia, Beaver, Norfolk, Ark Royal, Illustrious, Invincible, Battleaxe, Bristol, Boxer, Exeter, Trenchant, Diligence, Beaver, Fort George, Olwen, Sir Percivale, Chatham

SENIOR NAVAL OFFICERS IN HONG KONG

COMMODORE	DATE OF APPOINTMENT	COMMODORE	DATE OF APPOINTMENT
OJ JONES	1866-1869	CG SEDGWICK	1935-1937
JA PRICE	1869-1870	EBC DICKEN CBE DSC	1937-1939
FP SHORTT	1870-1873	AM PETERS DSC	1939-1940
JE PARISH	1873-1876	COMMANDER D CRAVEN	1940-1945
GW WATSON	1876-1879	DH EVERETT CBE DSO	1945-1947
TE SMITH	1879-1881	CL ROBERTSON	1947-1949
WH CUMING	1881-1884	LN BROWNFIELD CBE	1949-1951
GD MORANT	1884-1887	HG DICKINSON DSC	1951-1953
WH MAXWELL ADC	1887-1888	AH THOROLD OBE DSC	1953-1955
EJ CHURCH	1888-1891	JH UNWIN DSC	1955-1957
H St. LB PALLISTER	1891-1893	GDA GREGORY DSO	1957-1960
GTH BOYES	1893-1896	ARL BUTLER DSC	1960-1962
SC HOLLAND ADC	1896-1899	GO SYMONDS DSC	1962-1965
F POWELL CB	1899-1902	FD HOLFORD DSC	1965-1967
CG ROBINSON ADC	1902-1904	THP WILSON	1967-1968
CG DICKEN	1904-1905	PRC HIGHAM	1968-1970
HP WILLIAMS	1905-1907	RES WYKES-SNEYD	1970-1972
RHS STOKES	1907-1908	JK STEVENS	1972-1973
H LYON	1908-1910	JAG EVANS	1973-1975
CJ EYRES	1910-1912		
RH ANSTRUTHER CMG	1912-1916	CAPTAIN IN CHARGE	
HGG SANDEMEN CMG	1916-1918	RL GARNONS-WILLIAMS	1975-1978
VG GURNER	1918-1920	RW MOLAND	1978-1980
W BOWDEN SMITH CBE	1920-1922	AA WAUGH	1980-1982
HE GRACE	1922-1924	FA COLLINS	1982-1985
AJB STIRLING CB	1924-1926	CW GOTTO	1985-1987
JL PEARSON CMG	1926-1928	P DALRYMPLE-SMITH	1987-1990
RAS HILL	1928-1930	MC GORDON-LENNOX	1990-1991
AH WALKER	1930-1932	TLM SUNTER	1991-1994
E McC W LAWRIE	1932-1933		
HR MARRACK DSC	1933-1933	COMMODORE	
F ELLIOTT OBE	1933-1935	PJ MELSON CBE	1994-1997

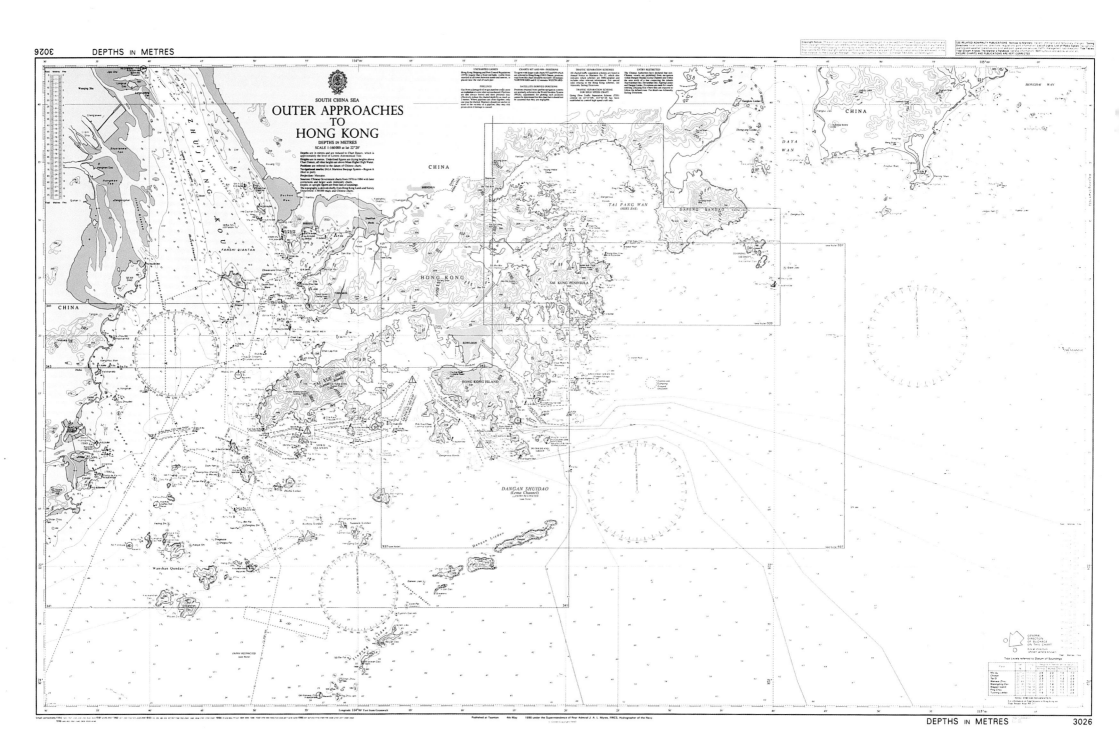

SOUTH CHINA SEA

OUTER APPROACHES TO HONG KONG

DEPTHS IN METRES

SCALE 1:160,000 at lat 22°20'